APPLA

"I've been waiting for this type
It's a new era and our collective time is now to have what I am with Christ in me."
April Hall, Storm Consultants LLC

"Jeff has been building a long time as a roofing general contractor. Now he is digging the foundation and pouring the essential concrete of character."
Mikki Willis, Film Producer, Plandemic

"I AM I HAVE," this book incorporates the essentials of living. Dealing with Character, Conflict, Courage and Confidence will catapult us to become overcomers."
Greg Brock, Beacon Materials

"Jeff has a passion for our industry and people being one mind and one voice to be all we can be so together we can win."
Paul Reed, Northwest Roofing

" In this book are the essential principles for life and business if you want to take it to the limit."
Troy Clymer, The Catalyst Group

"Success in business is directly correlated to keeping and honoring Jesus as Lord. Lord means 'boss over every area of life.' Keeping God first, then family, then business. That's Godly order and in doing so you walk in the "blessings of the Lord that maketh one rich."
Patty Cepeda, Isagenix, Top Income Earners Worldwide

"We have everything within ourselves to create everything it is we want out of life if we listen to the voice of wisdom and make right decisions. That's what this book means to me."
Ephriam Glick, Roofing Coatings

"If integrity is to be restored in the roofing industry it begins right here. Jeff unmasks the keys to making right decisions and living a God centered life to business."
Steve Patrick, Level the Playing Field

"It seems to be a spiritual truth that before a higher power can being to operate in your life you must first believe it he can. Faith is what's required. "

Paul Aragon, Jireh Roofing

"In our greatest moments of struggle, when all we want to do is do more in hopes of making it better, our best course of action is to be quiet and let God guide us. This book can be your guide for opening that channel to Gods guidance for the clarity, confidence and knowing right action we all seek to have as leaders."
Vicki Suiter, Suiter Business Builders, Author of The Profit Bleed

"My Dad (Jeff) has a burning desire to reform our industry to be all it can be to leave a legacy for future generations. Let it begin with a character shift for all in this

Dr. Jessica Stahl PHD, Ignite Results

"I go to bed each night and wake up each day going through a checklist of my head trying to make sure I did what I said. Actions speak louder than words. Following through with actions will always gain loyalty and trust. Yes this book is a must read."

Autumn Woosck, Storm Ventures Group

"Society is truly lacking class and character. We as women have the gift to carry class into the world and shine to be an example for our younger generation."

Kimberly Reed, Storm Gen Leads

"Jeff Richfield for decades has been a man of contagious prayer passion and action. It is a privilege to call him a friend and it is remarkable to see him seek the Lord and seek wisdom with such fervor. I believe this devotional will be extremely inspirational and helpful to all who are privileged to obtain it...there are life enhancing treasures found within…Enjoy!"

Pastor Scott MacLeod, Harvest Sound International

"Jeff has captured the heartbeat and the essence of developing character with the sword of the Word of God which does not EVER return void!!" Soak in this book like a sponge.

Mark Kouch, Author of The First Hour for Men

"As a life coach, I know the deeper your character the greater respect you cultivate winning long lasting relationship. It's our reputation that is at risk and this book will leave a fingerprint on your character for life."

Bill Maddox, Professional Performance Life Coach

Business Excellence Starts Here

I AM
I HAVE

Discovering Godly Character
as
Your New Bottom Line

A 40 DAY BUSINESS
APPLICATION JOURNAL

Jeff M. Richfield

I AM I HAVE - 40 Day Business Application Guide
By: Jeff M. Richfield

Richfield Publishing
admin@musiccityroofers.com
1-615-900-4000

Printed in the United States of America.

DEDICATION

I dedicate this book to those who have helped shape my character.

I honor my parents, beginning with my dad as my 'mentor of entrepreneurship.' He was a capitalist by every sense of the word. My mother, who was there steadfast in my growing years. She took me to positive therapy courses when I was only 10 years-old instilling in me the virtue of optimism. My brother Eric for his dependability, and always standing for me. My older brother Steve , who passed years ago, but was always supportive of me in my teenage years collaborating in music.

I'm thankful for my faithful friends, the men who continue to stand by my side to lead and guide me such as Onnie Kirk, my spiritual father for his wisdom. Then there's the persevering men of our prayer meetings from Tuesdays Table, Contractors Prayer Fellowship, Pastors from many churches like Scott Macleod for his dedication; my own employees from Music City Roofers who teach me the art of patience by chiseling all my grand visions into the one most important thing, obedience.

Most of all, it's my immediate family who teach me about character day by day. My wife, Jodi for her unwavering loyalty; you are my sunshine; for my two sons James, and Jacob, for their trustworthiness and obedience, and my mother-in-law, Juanita, who when I think of her I hear her playing those old gospel hymns on her baby grand piano while angels gaze.

Finally, in dedicating this work to readers worldwide my prayer is for the Great I AM to open your mind and personalize His message: "*Know Me as your habitation.*" That you can say, " I AM who You say I AM. I HAVE all You say I HAVE, and I DO what You call me to DO."

This is God's Great Reset. When we believe in Christ, His Spirit dwells in us so we have sonship-God's image sealed on our hearts. So as a son, we have what the Great I AM has. I dedicate the title of this book spoken to me by revelation through Baylor Wilson on February 24th, 2021.

"Commit your works to the Lord and your plans shall be established."

Proverbs 16:3

FORWARD

This book is a 40-day journey and personalized action plan for business owners, contractors, entrepreneurs, the men and women in the marketplace to develop and reshape the heartbeat of your company. We begin with the most critical character traits, define them, reflect on them, pray them, and then declare them out loud over your soul. In feeding your soul and spirit using the word of God, you transform your mind and soul to become your word, (so your life will flourish and your business will be all it is meant to be) to make the most impact in the world. This 40-day process will develop the heart of your company and if duly applied will bring transformation to you and your employees as well.

This business application guide is not only for business owners, but anyone working in the marketplace of all trades and industries. We're using a simple formula and proven technique that will equip, inspire and ignite and transform your heart and your mind to create new biblical belief patterns to make better, more wiser decisions to dismantle strongholds, and false belief patterns to fortify your spirit within and transform your thinking to create wiser decisions.

This small but mighty book is a 40-day reboot process to reshape your heart to carry a new wineskin for a new heartbeat for your company. By taking each day seriously using the instructions below:

- You will discover God's blueprint for business success
- You will discover the real you
- You will lose unhealthy habits
- You will form healthy habits
- You will discover you are who God says you are
- You will discover your real net worth-the gold in you

In the pages to follow, I've given you short daily bursts of God's word. He is the "I AM." And as I carry His word, "You HAVE" what it declares, and His word shall not return void. It shall perform what it is sent to do! You can believe and declare, "I AM who You say I AM!

PREFACE

We are living in dark times. What was once good and righteous in our country is now being considered as evil. Is this the "new normal?"

What does this mean for you and your business? How can you lead your people well and walk with a renewed sense of confidence in stride and achieve more than ever before with such division and unrest socially, politically, and economically?

As an owner of a small to medium sized organization you can only lead well if you're armed well. We give you the best tools to win and be successful. First, we will discuss your key to transformative power by receiving the Light, your "GOD WHY" in life. How do we reach our goals if we don't know what our unique "Why" is or know what we are called to be? The truth is we each have what I call a "unique identifying purpose," a calling within which defines our "GOD WHY."

It is my belief that your unique calling and purpose has already been predetermined by our divine Creator. Your mission if you are willing to take it is to look deep within to realize your dignity and honor; to stand in authority of your position on earth, and take the land before you to demonstrate what the Kingdom of God looks like on earth.

The Battle is the Lords and He has given You the Keys to Win

Whether you've been a Christian for many year's or have just recently given your Life to Jesus, or do not yet know Him at all - in either case this book is for you. The Word of God declares when we accept Jesus in our life we are Kings and Priests who shall rule in the earth. As a business owner you're in the marketplace five days a week to develop your team, serve your clients, and be an example of light and love to others. That's how we take the land. Make no mistake, we are in a battle on earth and we have a real enemy named, satan. His fallen angels do not want you to succeed and flourish. We cannot be unaware of his tactics. Therefore, we are to put on our spiritual armor daily.
WAR in the spirit by applying these three essentials each morning:
W- Be **WASHED** in the blood, A- **ARMOR** up: put on your armor of Ephesians 6, and finally, R - **REFILL** in the spirit each morning. Mark Kouch shared this with me, and I use "WAR" daily to say "NO" to the enemy.

The Next Great Revival Will Stem from the Marketplace

Again, we are living in dark times. Division and distraction are methods our enemy choses to destroy and conquer businessmen and women who have a calling to innovate and be wealth providers who transform their communities by providing a livelihood to the workforce.

As a Christian business owner in a growing industry, you and your employees are all part of a larger conglomerate of light-bearer's to be salt on the earth. To beat the odds and dark spiritual forces operating against us we need to develop our character to make each one of us stronger in faith to transform our businesses and our communities. We do each other a great disservice in being apathetic to the deeper calling of God at work in the marketplace. We cannot go at it and walk alone anymore.

Woe to Those Who call Good Evil and Evil Good.

It's a sad fact, what was once considered good and righteous in our country is now being considered as wrong and evil. Isaiah 5:20 speaks of such a time warning, "Woe those who call evil good, and good evil; who put darkness for light and light for darkness." Men and women of God, it's time we stand and group together like never before. Daily now we are seeing the rise of injustice and unrighteousness at work. If the soul of America's freedom and Constitution are on the line then it's only a matter of time our 'business faith' will be threatened also. We must unite to keep the sanctity of moral business ethics and stand waving our flag for the American Dream-Entrepreneurial Liberty with an Enduring Business Owner-shift.

Making Owner-Shift Essential as Our New Normal

An Owner-Shift is what I define as a Mind-shift. It is simply a redeveloping of our character. The worlds plumb-line of moral code has shifted. What was once called right is wrong. Truth is not black and white anymore. Our way forward is to guard our hearts by meditating on God's Word, for out of it flows the issues of life. We are commanded to constantly renew our mind and take every thought captive. For the discerning, the wheel of character is a continual lifestyle. (See the Wheel of Godly Character at the rear of this book).

Jesus, (Yeshua) declared Himself to be the Truth and the Light. He is the Truth-plumbline of our doctrine. Therefore, our decisions must be spiritually motivated and displayed by a conscious display of Godly character.

The good news is the Good News is already at work. Men and women of the light are grouping together like never before building communities within to be an integrated expression of faith, and a courageous body determined to be the voice of the free and the brave.

In keeping of what our Lord commanded we "take up our cross" and follow Jesus. Jesus was a man of deep character who walked His talk. In meekness, He was a man surrendered to His Father's will fulfilling the ultimate eternal exchange through obedience to the very end. If we are to be more like Him, and become better leaders in our companies and communities, it's time we put on integrity and humility and step up to the challenges lying before us.

Building a spiritual business community within the corporate world is a natural offshoot of spiritual practice within the four walls of the church. The marketplace is a second family where spiritually minded conduct business daily. The spiritual workplace is where brothers and sisters gain strength in prayer to overcome; where the isolated are heard; where business owners gain wisdom and become better stewards to build an enduring culture and leave behind a legacy for the next generation.

We are the called, believing God for revival and spiritual breakthrough in the marketplace. Strong spiritual fathers and mothers are needed to sacrifice time for young entrepreneurs to discover their spiritual roots. As one "new man" a reformation of character is the stage for the great end time harvest to come; one of epic proportions I call, "God's Great Reset." In biblical terminology this is, "The Great Commission."

Why Should I Read and Practice this Book?

If you want to put God at work and see the miraculous this book is for you. If you sense your integrity is lacking and you need air support this book is for you. If you need consistency in sharpening your skills in using the Word of God as your sword this book is for you. If you desire courage to stand against the devil in the workplace and in life, then this book is for you. If your desire is to simply grow in your prayer life and increase your faith, then for all these reasons and many more this book is for you.

Know that God wants His light to come into your business. He wants you to have a testimony that will out-shine your losses, your burials, your depression, and your fears to be the God of resurrection life to share with others.

Contained in this small but mighty book are not merely words on a page, but an action plan packed into a 40-day journey to journal the transformations of your heart, your family, and your workplace.

40 Days to Develop a New Wineskin - A New You

One cannot hold new wine in an old wineskin. Jesus declared Himself in Mark 2:22, "No one pours new wine into old wineskins. For the wine would burst the wineskins; new wine calls for new wineskins." The Lord gave me a picture of the new wineskin I call, "The Wheel of Character," shown in the rear of this book. It begins with and P.U.SH. (Pray until something happens) then Salvation! Spiritual rebirth is needed before you can grasp the ideas this book contains, and prayer is how we maintain a relationship beyond words. It is the primary expression of the life we have in Christ in our mortal bodies. This book contains daily bread to maximize your prayers and make your business make sense.

Each day of this journey equips you with character definitions, declarations to pray, and reflections to journal. Using the sword of the Word of God, these daily declarations will reshape your thinking to create new habits of success. This book taken seriously will literally transform your heart to hold new revelations of character skills which will help you overcome and be more compassionate toward your family, fruitful with your employees, and patient with your clients. If you allow God to go with you to work and through your life, He will bring all things together, and you will look back ten years from now like me and see how He carried you each step of the way through. Having sacrificed His life for you, He can be trusted to see you all the way through. Trust in the Word of life.

Most Business Owners Make Money More Than Impact

Before we get started helping you and your company be the best it can be, I want you to make the distinction "why" you're doing what you're doing. I made the decision early on I wanted my career to be my calling. Ask yourself, "what is my plan with all this money I'll make?" God's desire is for you to walk in relationship with Him and to make Him known at work. Trust me, you will want to be certain you are driven to the right purpose and pursuit. If you truly want to find providence and fulfillment and validation and reputation, follow my lead here.

The Bible teaches us a world of wisdom about work but, first in seeking His Kingdom...

"But seek ye first the kingdom of God and His righteousness and all these things will be added to you." Matthew 6:33

"These things" are riches, honor, and life. This is only one morsel of God's wisdom at work. But how do we share our faith at work?

"We will take our faith to work only if we know that our work is valuable to God." - Ken Costa

A New Definition of Success

We want to begin by saying the first thing in seeking God's kingdom is our search for a Godly character. What speaks most about us as we relate to other people is the character that we portray and leave behind. There is no sense in having a business when we cannot keep our word, or we argue with others frequently, or we have a sense of arrogance about us. In the paragraphs below we will explore important character attributes so we can be living examples in the marketplace.

As you journey with us through the next 40 days, I've outlined character traits and given their definition. We share other's experiences and provide hope for change with a daily declaration to state your new belief out loud. Finally, you will end your session with a space for journaling your experiences.

Meditation, Prayer, and Journaling as a Life-Long Pursuit

Meditation, prayer ,and journaling has become part of my daily bread. I have a recorded library of over 20+ years of pages filled with experiences from the dark night of my soul such as recovering from my stroke, the loss of family members and animals, entire business losses gone in a blink. But those experiences prepared me for the best days of my life with God at work: writing about the joys of business success, relationships restored, books written, prayers that moved hearts, my years in recovery, my first real estate flip making over $350,000.00, and the love, forgiveness and acceptance of my family as we grow in patience; this life truly is a wonderful life!

Through the maze of life, I've come to realize how the Lord, Jesus, has been my guiding light each step through the valley. I have become more confident with a new faith that liberates me from paralyzing challenges, fears, past-pains and addictions, and character problems. I look back and see the Good Shepherd's rod at work and how His fingerprint has marked my life over the years.

I also learned to make healthy habits. Using reflections and declarations with the Holy Spirit as my witness, I am continuing to learn how to 'walk full' in the spirit, renew my mind, altar negativity to His light and love to find a new authenticity. How do I do this?

Work-Ship! The Doorway to Authority and Strength

In each of the 40-days you'll want to maximize your efforts by developing a healthy habit of diet and exercising as part of your daily regimen. Your job is to make sure you workout in some fashion six days a week. I've come up with my own unique system of using weightlifting or running and combine it with worshiping God. I call it "Work-Ship." The neat thing is the bible declares, "The joy of the Lord is our strength." So it stands to reason that when I need strength I'll worship God. I find joy works 100% of the time. If you want my song play-list just tag me on Facebook or email me, and I'll send it.

I cannot stress it LOUD enough! You need to take good care of our MIND, BODY, and SPIRIT! As a believer YOU have authority to create and rule your world. Believe it is so by faith in Work-Ship!

These four factors are how I win each day. *Prayer and journaling*; where I hear God's heart and Counsel for wisdom; then *fill my body* with the right blend of healthy eating. Next is *Work-Ship*, to strengthen my spirit and body, and finally, *Goals*- my workday plan. This is how I get refilled each day, and at 57 yrs old I still feel like I'm 25 yrs young. This is how the water of life flows continually where the river never runs dry!

A Word on Acts of Service and Compassion at Work

Selfless service and compassion is of great importance in the home and workplace. It may be the very best way to show our love for others. It is the laying down of ones life for another the Lord speaks about in the book of John, 15:13 that speaks of selfless service. This love comes in all the tiny instances we are afforded each day to show compassion on our way and at work. These tiny acts come from hearing the quiet voice and obeying. We are all afforded these small important moments each day as we hear and obey and afterward confirmed from the validation of our Father.

At my company, we pray for God's blessings at company wide meetings, and I recall an occasion , said a prayer over their life, and they opened up confessing their sin and cried out to God for salvation. Taking time to engage with your employees and empathize with their needs are opportunities to show respect and kindness and we shall see another soul come to the kingdom.

Compassion could be giving praise to one of my employees who had a victory or is suffering from things unsaid. Selfless service is about having your plan for the day but not letting your plan supersede a genuine need. As a leader at work be listening and mindful of others. As a owner I strive to push others up the ladder to better communicate. Spending quality time weekly with each core member hearing their heart and meeting their needs as an act of service and compassion go hand in hand. The Lord promises not to forget even a glass of water given to another. So do well in the small things.

"And if anyone gives even a cup of cold water to one of these little ones who is my disciple, truly I tell you, that person will certainly not lose their reward."
Matthew 10:42

INTRODUCTION

Redefining Our Character

I am part of a nationwide men's prayer group in the roofing industry called, Contractors Fellowship. Coach Jim Johnson started this group years ago and it's developing into a safe haven where men can share and know their prayers matter and are heard. We pray weekly and are convicted and commissioned to be a voice to re-define, redevelop, and strengthen our community by discovering Godly character in the marketplace. As followers of Christ, we see this industry-wide impasse that can only be cured by another great awakening. Our ambitions are simply, His will be done on earth as it is in heaven!

To share how powerful the Lord works through prayer, on one of our early morning Wednesday calls we had an epiphany relating to the great need for a resurgence of character growth.

The 5 C's - Five Key Areas of Great Need

The following conversations were taken from our prayer group in February of 2021. I wrote it down because it was the same day the Lord was speaking to me about character and inviting me to write this book.

My friend's Jim, Reggie, Nathan, and a few others put it like this:

"When considering the scripture, "Seek first the Kingdom of God, then all the other things will be added unto you." Most People make a choice to get what they want and seek the other things. Consider who you are, and what do you want? "Those things" have an impact on who we are and what we desire. Consider, that the Fruits of the spirit will fall from me naturally when I am walking in the spirit. Let us pray first to hunger and thirst for righteousness rather than getting "all the other things." The point is if we first pray to become the thing that gets us the promises, we get the promises as a guarantee from God's word. So, Seek first the kingdom of God, then all other things come." Credit to Coach Nathan Tebedo.

A Book Was Being Born

As we engaged, I got a vivid picture like I had when I authored my last book of how God was wanting to get this message out to the workplace. Reggie and Jim also shared how we must examine our motives to get the right outcome. We came up with these five key areas needing attention.

1. **Character redefinition.** Do personal inventory with work-life. Be rigorously honest with yourself and evaluate your situation.
2. **Conflict resolution.** Determine how to handle conflict on the job. Situations arise where we need to know how to handle pressures.
3. **Courage.** Courage is saying no to others of influence who want to compromise our virtues. Fear of Loss makes us choose wrong. Be willing to surrender your way to God's or peers ways.
4. **Confidence.** We hear about arrogance in our industry. We can control outcome through the ability to choose. If you want to develop character, there's no need to prove your confidence.
5. **Choice.** Once we develop character everything else falls in line. We determined much of our growth starts with decisions, and our choices really do control our future.

These themes became building blocks for the book you are reading. God suggested I turn these into 40-days of character-building exercises to redefine our lives and businesses beginning with one simple decision. You now hold in your hands what was written in 40 days.

Earlier that day I had been reading in Exodus 28:30. This passage jumped out at me like lightning about Aaron, the priest, and how he came before the Lord daily, *"to bare the decisions for Israel that his heart would be the Lord's heart for them."*

Our decision making drives our future. We long for your heart to be the Lords heart for our industry. We need God's help to hold our hearts like Aaron. So we pray, *"Holy Spirit, help us make decisions like Aaron as kings and priests you've called us to be!"*

Do You Struggle with Excessive Internal Dialogue?

Many of our external struggles come from duplicity of thinking. We live in a world filled with double-mindedness and fear. What drives us is the internal over-thinking that if not taken into captivity can have us going every which way but true north! Our instability can only be reckoned with by removing the garbage inside our hearts and being filled entirely with the Holy Spirit. We have freedom of choice and must take responsibility with our actions.

This action is "to take every thought into captivity to Christ," and by putting on the new mind of peace. If you are being tormented by excessive thoughts, speak the peace of Jesus' words over your mind right now: Pray. *"Lord, grant me peace in my mind and heart."*

"My Peace I leave with you; my peace I give you. I do not give to you as the world gives. Do not let your hearts be troubled and do not be afraid." John 14:27

PUT OFF ungodliness and PUT ON Godly character

From Colossians 3:1-17, we are exhorted to PUT OFF:
"If then you were raised with Christ, seek those things which are above, where Christ is, sitting at the right hand of God. Set your mind on things above, not on things on the earth. "For you died, and your life is hidden with Christ in God. When Christ who is our life appears, then you also will appear with Him in glory."

"Therefore, put to death your members which are on the earth: fornication, uncleanness, passion, evil desire, and covetousness, which is idolatry. Because of these things the wrath of God is coming upon the sons of disobedience, in which you yourselves once walked when you lived in them."

"But now you yourselves are to put off all these: anger, wrath, malice, blasphemy, filthy language out of your mouth. Do not lie to one another, since you have put off the old man with his deeds, and have put on the new man who is renewed in knowledge according to the image of Him who created him, where there is neither Greek nor Jew, circumcised nor uncircumcised, barbarian, Scythian, slave nor free, but Christ is all and in all."

Reflecting further from Colossians 3, we are to PUT ON fruitfullness:

"Therefore, as the elect of God, holy and beloved, put on tender mercies, kindness, humility, meekness, longsuffering; bearing with one another, and forgiving one another, if anyone has a complaint against another; even as Christ forgave you, so you also must do. But above all these things put on love, which is the bond of perfection. And let the peace of God rule in your hearts, to which also you were called in one body; and be thankful. Let the word of Christ dwell in you richly in all wisdom, teaching and admonishing one another in psalms and hymns and spiritual songs, singing with grace in your hearts to the Lord. And whatever you do in word or deed, do all in the name of the Lord Jesus, giving thanks to God the Father through Him." Colossians 3:1-17

Time to Take Inventory

Jesus' Word and His Holy Spirit must be ALIVE inside your spirit for this book to have lasting transformation on the outside. The Father set it up that we need to repent to receive. Repentance is a serious matter. The Bible teaches there is a literal hell and worse yet, there is a Hell conspiracy you must be aware of. Satan just needs a little unforgiveness to keep you from heaven, but the Good News is we can have access to Heaven by turning our will over to Jesus as our Lord and Savior. The Bible says in Romans 10:13, *"Whomever calls upon the Name of the Lord shall be saved."* His name is Jesus, (Yeshua) the Christ.

Here is the bottom line. The steps below share how you can be saved, and know if you died today you would be going to heaven:

1. **Agree with God**. His Son, Jesus is the only Way to salvation.
2. **Have Godly Sorrow**. Your sin hurts Jesus' heart. Turn from it.
3. **Confess Sin**. Plead the Blood of Christ over you which saves your soul from a literal hell and washes you clean from sin.
4. **Put a New Standard in Place**. Do what you need to do to stop sinning. Start a recovery program? Turn off Facebook? Create a new diet? Tie a string around your finger as a reminder? But get in the Word of God daily each morning and keep on being filled, so the Holy Spirit is constantly carried with you.
5. **Repentance is the only acceptable sacrifice for your sin**. If you desire to see Jesus when you die and go to heaven, say this sinner's prayer, have faith in His saving grace, and make Him Lord of your life right now.

If you are ready to do business God's Way say this prayer in faith:

"Thank you, Lord for the ultimate sacrifice, Your Son, Jesus Christ (Yeshua). Wash me in the blood of Jesus. I want no part of hiding my sin. Change me. I believe you are the Son of the living God. I forgive myself and hold no root of bitterness for others. Please Forgive me Lord and send me Your Holy Spirit to fill me up. I forgive everyone

I've held bitterness toward. Hell is not worth my unforgiveness. Thank you for saving my soul. Now redefine my character and stamp Your image on my life. Give me an outpouring of Your Holy Spirit. I trust You to finish the work You've begun. In Jesus name I pray."

CONGRATULATIONS!! Now if you prayed that prayer in faith, you've just become a new spirit inside. And you will experience a new desire to live a clean righteous life. But, you'll need some help in accountability with Godly men and women to become disciplined. Cease doing the things you know hurts you and our industry from being a light which brightens our reputation. Make it a daily habit to read your Bible each morning. Be sure to reach out to my staff and we can help you on the journey.

By following this 40-day action plan I guarantee you will experience a new level of transformation which will roll into your business. Now you can take this book for granted and have a minimum life-change experience or dive deep like others who have applied these principles daily in their lives, and have gained deeper insight, new perspectives, experience, strength, and hope.

Finally, as you read, know you have been prayed for to know the love of Christ which passes knowledge; that you may be filled with all the fullness of God. *"Now to Him who is able to do exceedingly abundantly above all that we ask or think, according to the power that works in us, to Him be glory in the church by Christ Jesus to all generations, forever and ever. Amen. "*

Ephesians 3:14-21

"Nothing short of a new Pentecost and outpouring of the Spirit that brings newness, creativity, and adventure is required if we are to see our places of work transformed, our communities thriving with life, and our society healed." -Ken Costa

The Holy Spirit Shows Us Our Blind Spots

We all have blind spots. Jesus came to earth, *"...to give sight to the blind eye to show those who might think they can see that they are really blind,"* John 9:39. I love that wisdom. Hes' not talking about physical blindness here, but He came to earth to show us our blind spots so we can see ourselves as who we really are. This is foundational in seeking Godly character. Even King David asked the Lord, in Psalm 19:12, *"But who can discern their own errors? Forgive my hidden faults."* So ask for clarity. Know when your thoughts aren't lined up for success you can ask the Lord and others for help.

Pray the prayer David prayed. *"Deliver me Lord from hidden flaws."* It can be a scary thought that none of us can see our own errors, but here is the Good News: *We can and need to ask for His help and grace when we fail.*

"We want to be free of all delusions and deceptions; not just the fake news and values in the world, but the ones we have deep within our own hearts."

The Capsule of God's Faithfulness

NOTE: DO NOT GIVE UP HOPE IF YOU FAIL!

God promises us four ways He is faithful to see us through our journey in bearing Godly character. We aren't faithful to fully live out the real christian life without the Holy Spirit's continual refilling.

#1. He gives us the Helper when we fail. "He will never leave nor forsake us." Hebrews 13:5
#2. When we fail or sin. "He is faithful and just to forgive us and cleanse us from all unrighteousness." 1 John 1:9
#3. God is faithful. "He will not allow you to be tempted more than you can bear but He will provide a way out." 1 Corinthians 10:13
#4. Be anxious for nothing. "...but by everything pray...and the peace of God, which passes ALL understanding will guard your hearts and minds through Christ Jesus." Philippians 4:7
This is our Good News pill: God's faithfulness always outlasts our shortcomings. I call it His capsule of faith. Take it daily on an empty stomach!

Note to self: DEVELOP A LISTENING HEART

As you take this forty-day spiritual journey, have your pen ready to journal. You'll want to pause and listen for the Holy Spirit speak to you. God's spirit is actively at work and has ideas to share for your day. He will prompt you if you're open to receive. You will hear Him speak ever so softly, even as a whisper. Write down what you hear and like I mentioned before one day you'll look back and see the footprints of Jesus who carried you each step of the way.

If you're ready to start, pause and say this short prayer with me:

'Father God, I come to You in Your Sons name, and ask for the spirit of wisdom and revelation to be released over my mind. Let my thoughts come into alignment with Your will so that my plans are established and succeed. Develop the areas of my life that need character building and remove the bad habits which hold me from seeing your work in my business. I now open the door and welcome Your Holy Spirit to be Boss of my business. Help me step back and see God @ work in my workplace to be the best leader I can be for my people. In Jesus name. Amen." OKAY. Turn the page for Day One on your journey!

Instructions for Journaling

In each of the 40-days I want you to use your words to dictate your future using declarations of faith. A daily reflection given in the journal uses the acronym, 'H A V E' for you to write an expression in the following manner:

What do I **HAVE** gratitude for…(meditate on todays character trait)
What am I **ASPIRING** toward…(Your character goal for today is...)
Where I had **VICTORY** today…(relating to your key word)
What am I **EXPECTING** in faith to do today using my key word...
(What I plan to do today as an action using todays character trait)

Journaling will provide a clearing ground for your emotions to get the inside out, express passion to God for new character, share sorrow and joy in failure and victory, and put the lid on it. When you close your journal your day is set to win. OKAY. READY. SET. GO!

Turn the page....Your best days begin NOW!

Day 1

I AM THE LIGHT

"LIGHT" is defined as

1. The natural agent that stimulates sight and makes things visible. An expression in someone's eyes indicating a particular emotion or mood

---

"Character is being OK making mistakes. Mistakes are human and never really the issue. The response to the mistake is what reveals your character. Be the light!"

-John Dye, American Contractor Summit

> Note:
> You must have a deep faith and strong sense of belief in your declaration; or it is merely words on paper making no transformation at all. Rather, the words must jump out as the ink would spill out all over your soul and leave its mark stamped and sealed as your new mantra or new self image in Christ.

I DECLARE,

I HAVE THE LIGHT living inside me.

You are the Great I AM, the Light of my life. I walk in the fullness of Your Living Word. I am made in God's image so we are in this together. Darkness must flee! It is my time to let God's love-light shine through me. I declare God's supernatural light into my life and business is now active. I let God's loving-light loose in my life and business. Today, I am filled with light and have the power of heaven to advance the Kingdom of God on earth. This is my declaration. So be it. **Amen.**

Reflection – Let your having become your doing...

Light travels at over 186,282 miles per second. Scientists claim light is moving faster and faster as our universe expands. Being the light in this world means being a light-bearer; one who expands the love of God to others. *WHY?* He wants to give you a testimony that outshines your loss, your burials, your depression. When you see the invisible ALL is possible. His resurrection power will bring healing in its wings. Reflect on your life and ask how you can let your light shine brighter in your present darkness. Consider what you can do to shine brighter in your workplace today. Give time to meditate and journal.

Having Gratitude for LIGHT:________________________________

____

Aspiring goals for being the LIGHT today:______________________

____

Victory I celebrated yesterday being the LIGHT:__________________

____

Expecting in Faith for having LIGHT:___________________________

____

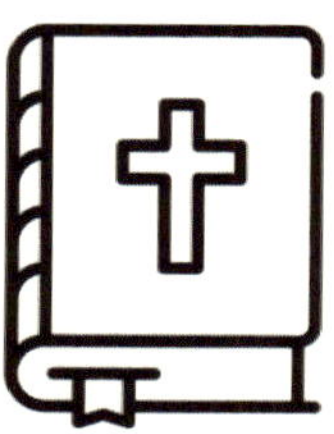	**My Day 1 Character Builder** *"I pray that the eyes of your heart may be enlightened so that you will know what is the hope of His (Gods) calling and what are the riches of the glory of His inheritance in the saints."* Ephesians1:18

Day 2

I AM YOUR FINGERPRINT

Noun

1. An impression or mark made on a surface by a person's fingertip, especially as used for identifying individuals from the unique pattern of whorls and lines.

"Fingerprints are God's marks on human hands. An artist discovered there were 66 lines in the fingerprint. To his great surprise, He realized this was the exact same number of books in the bible so he wrote a scripture for each line and came up with a picture that sells online to share God's truth of who we each are - divinely knit and crafted into spiritual creatures on earth." – Jason Van Dyke

I DECLARE,

I HAVE THE FINGERPRINT of God on my fingers.

Your Spirit is living and active in me. Each day is a new beginning on my journey of intimacy with You. I carry the treasure of Your glory in my heart, and the fire of your works in my hands to create my unique special purpose. These hands were made to greet and be a blessing to every person I meet. I share Your message with the world. I am fearfully and wonderfully made. Today, I am blessed coming in and have the blessings of God going out to work. This is my declaration. So be it. **Amen.**

Reflection – Let your having become your doing...

Only God could be smart enough to make over seven billion humans all with a unique mark. In what ways will you leave your unique impact and blessing in the marketplace for the world to see? Take a look at your hands and fingers and express gratitude that you're one of a kind.

Having Gratitude for:____

____

Aspiring Goals for today:_____________________________________

____

Victory I celebrated yesterday:_________________________________

____

Expecting in Faith for:______________________________________

____

My Day 2 Character Builder

"For You formed my inward parts; You covered me in my mother's womb. I will praise You, for I am fearfully and wonderfully made; Marvelous are Your works, And that my soul knows very well. My frame was not hidden from You, When I was made in secret, And skillfully wrought in the lowest parts of the earth." Psalm 139:13-15

Day 3

I AM SALVATION

Noun

1. Deliverance from sin and its consequences, believed by Christians to be brought about by faith in Christ.

"Saved by Grace alone means that God loves, forgives, and saves us not because of who we are or what we do, but because of the work of Christ. Our salvation is in God's hands. The evidence of our salvation is what's happening in us now and the fruit we produce. Jesus gives every believer the Holy Spirit, which gives us a desire to live for God - the ability to hear, recognize and respond to God's voice." Jeff Richfield

If You gave your life to Christ, you should declare with confidence:

I DECLARE,
I HAVE SALVATION.

I am born again. I have the Spirit of Christ living in me. The love of God has been shed abroad in me by the Holy Spirit. It is no longer I that live but Christ who lives in me. Greater is He Who is in me than he that is in the world. God is for me and nothing can stand against me. Today, I am doing all things through Christ and have His strength in me. This is My declaration. So be it. **Amen**.

Reflection-Let your having become your doing...

Have you given your life to Jesus? Do you employees have a relationship with Christ? Are you willing to begin praying for your employees daily for the Holy Spirit to come into their lives? I have added my daily company prayer in the back of the book for you to see an example. Write a prayer of gratitude for your employees or your boss below. This is your "doing" of your "having."

Have Gratitude for SALVATION:____________________________

____

Aspiring Goals for today: _________________________________

____

Victory I celebrated yesterday:_____________________________

____

Expecting in Faith for:__________________________________

____

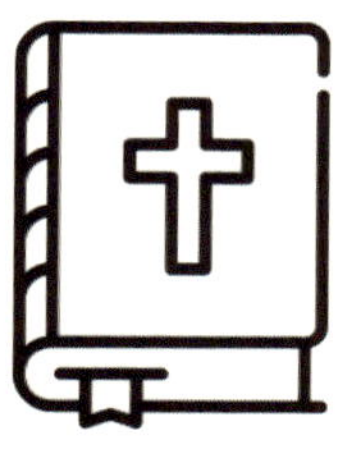

My Day 3 Character Builder

"For I am not ashamed of the gospel of Christ, for it is the power of God to salvation for everyone who believes." "For the Son of Man has come to seek and to save that which was lost. Truly my soul silently waits for God; From Him comes my salvation." Romans 1:16, Luke 19:10, Psalm 62:1

Day 4

I AM HONEST

Adjective

1. Free of deceit and untruthfulness. Sincere. The quality of telling the truth after you did something wrong,

"Be honest with yourself first. You might think you can get away with it, that nobody will ever know, but that is just wishful thinking. You will always know when you are dishonest, and God will always convict you."

-Daniel Bolton, Sales Manager, Music City Roofers

I DECLARE,
I HAVE HONESTY.

I rise early to declare Your Lordship over my tongue and my eyes. I make the commitment to be honest and keep my eyes looking straight ahead not wavering to the left or right. I am not double-minded but single focused keeping my trust in Him knowing He will not fail me. I speak words of life and healing to my family and coworkers. Truthfulness and righteousness surround me as a shield as I keep my eyes on Jesus. Today, I am a partaker of God's divine nature and have honesty within me. This is my declaration. So be it. **Amen**.

Reflection – Let your having become your doing...

Jot down the last time you have been tempted to cheat and share how you tripped up or overcame it? We all fail, but the Lord is faithful to forgive us when we confess our transgressions. So Let's Get Real.

Have Gratitude for HONESTY:______________________________

____

Aspiring Goals for today:__________________________________

____

Victory I celebrated yesterday:_____________________________

____

Expecting in Faith for:____________________________________

____

____

	**My Day 4 Character Builder** *"The Lord abhors dishonest scales, but accurate weights are his delight. Study to show thyself approved unto God, a workman that needeth not to be ashamed, rightly dividing the word of truth."* Proverbs 11:1, 2 Timothy 2:5

Day 5

I AM FAITHFUL

Adjective

1. Complete trust or confidence in someone or something. Having a strong belief in God, based on spiritual apprehension rather than proof

It seems to be a spiritual truth, that before a higher power can begin to operate in your life, you must first believe that He can. God is saying, "Don't sweat the small stuff. Have faith, stay close to Me." -Paul Aragon, Jireh 7 Enterprises Roofing

I DECLARE,

I HAVE FAITH.

Lion of Judah ROAR! My God given destiny is inevitable! I choose faith over fear because my God is here. Greater is He who is in me than he who is in the world. I will experience God's faithfulness as I step out over the bridge of faith to my promised land. My mind is set on what God says about me. I am more than a conqueror in Christ! I am not moved by what I see. Today, I am walking by faith and not by sight. I have increased my faith now! This is my declaration. So be it. **Amen.**

Reflection – Let your having become your doing...

Faith is acting like it is so even when it isn't so, in order that it might be so, simply because He said so. What you have known and what you have become hinders you from what you can become. Faith in action releases risk. As you look over the horizon what steps do you have to take before you to grow faith? Who can you ask for help for wisdom in your decision?

Have Gratitude for FAITH:______________________________

____

Aspiring Goals for today:________________________________

____

Victory I celebrated yesterday:____________________________

____

Expecting in Faith for:_________________________________

____

	**My Day 5 Character Builder** *"Have faith in God,' Jesus answered. 'I tell you the truth. If anyone says to this mountain, 'Go, throw yourself into the sea, and does not doubt in his heart but believes that what he says will happen, it will be done for him. Therefore, I tell you, whatever you ask for in prayer, believe."* Mark 11:22

Day 6

I AM SURRENDERED

Noun

1. to cease resistance to an enemy or opponent and submit to their authority. To give up the right to be right.

"A lifetime of self-will run riot can come to a screeching halt, and change forever, by making a simple decision to surrender and turn it all over to God."

-Heath Hicks, AVCO Roofing

I DECLARE,
I HAVE SURRENDERED.

In Jesus name, I am now a new creation in Christ. I surrender my mind, my will, and emotions to the Holy Spirit. He is my eternal guide now. I receive heavenly instructions to illumine my way. God's Word is a lamp to my feet and a light to my path. I surrender the many voices within and chose to hear the Father speak as I obey. I let go and let God. Today, I am alive in Christ, surrendered to God's will, and let Jesus live BIG in me. I have surrendered. This is my declaration. So be it. **Amen**.

Reflection – Let your having become your doing...

There is a saying that whatever we resist will persist. On the other side of surrendering is the clearing for what is ready for you. Practice letting go of the areas of life you are not at peace with. Jesus, is our example, "Saying, Father, if thou be willing, remove this cup from Me, nevertheless not My will, but Yours be done." What "cross" do you need to pick up or let go of to get to your next destination?

Have Gratitude for SURRENDERING:________________________

____

Aspiring Goals for today:_________________________________

____

Victory I celebrated yesterday:____________________________

____

Expecting in Faith for:___________________________________

____

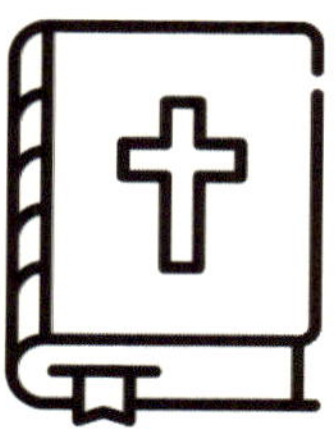

My Day 6 Character Builder

"I have been crucified with Christ; and it is no longer I who live, but Christ lives in me; and the life which I now live in the flesh I live by faith in the Son of God, who loved me and gave Himself up for me." Galatians 2:20

Day 7

I AM COURAGE

Noun

1. The ability to act while facing fear; strength in the face of pain, fear or grief.

"There is a saying that you can't change the spots on a leopard, but you can change the direction he walks. Turning from fear to courage is a process, not an event. The more I practice courage the more my true nature will be revealed."

April Hall, Founder, SRC Summit

I DECLARE,
I HAVE COURAGE.

I command the day to align with God's plan for my life. At twilight my enemies flee! I carry the presence of the Lord into my workplace today and take on the armor of courage to displace any and all fears. Lack does not threaten me. No harm can touch me. I am strong in the Lord and in the power of His might! I give birth to every dream God put in my heart. I am an overcomer by the blood of the Lamb and the word of my testimony. Today, I AM redeemed from the hand of the enemy to live courageously in the land I am given. This is my declaration. So be it. **Amen.**

Reflection – Let your having become your doing...

Courage is a door that can only be opened on the inside. There are seasons in life we feel we need to walk further to get further. Where do you feel the weakest so that God can be stronger to perform His work in you today?

Have Gratitude for COURAGE:______________________________

____

Aspiring Goals for today:___________________________________

____

Victory I celebrated yesterday:_______________________________

____

Expecting in Faith for:_____________________________________

____

____

	**My Day 7 Character Builder** *"Be strong and of good courage, do not fear nor be afraid of them; for the LORD your God, He is the One who goes with you."* Deuteronomy 31:6

Day 8

I AM INTEGRITY

Noun

1. the state of being whole and undivided. the quality of having strong moral principles; uprightness

---

"My shortcomings are there to provide the greatest opportunity for growth."
-Elias Raber, Conklin Roofing Coach

I DECLARE,

I HAVE INTEGRITY. I commit to take appropriate action today to be my best self in Christ.

I speak words of life and victory over myself, and my co-workers today. I am blessed within and blessed without. I am casting down vain imaginations. I guard my heart for out of it flows the issues of life. I am anointed and empowered by the creator of the universe. Lord, defend me from evil spirits who try to rise up against me! Enemies flee! Protect my integrity Oh God. Today, I shall be true to myself and do nothing to grieve the Holy Spirit. I have integrity. This is my declaration. So be it. **Amen.**

Reflection – Let your having become your doing...

Following the golden rule teaches us to treat others how you want to be treated. How is the spirit prompting you to pay attention to how you speak and treat others? We shall be judged by our words and actions. Do you have a problem interrupting others by allowing technology to interrupt conversations? How can you change your behavior?

Have Gratitude for INTEGRITY:______________________________

____

Aspiring Goals for today:____________________________________

____

Victory I celebrated yesterday:_________________________________

____

Expecting in Faith for:______________________________________

____

	**My Day 8 Character Builder** *"Let your eyes look straight ahead; fix your gaze directly before you. Give careful thought to the paths for your feet and be steadfast in all your ways. Do not turn to the right or the left; keep your foot from evil. People with integrity walk safely, but those who follow crooked paths will slip and fall."* Proverbs 4:25-27, Proverbs 10:9

Day 9

I AM ACCEPTANCE

Noun

1. the action of consenting to receive or undertake something offered

---

"One of my keys to spiritual growth is accepting character defects exactly as they are and becoming entirely willing to let them go. This applies to business too! Once I accept myself, I can learn to accept others."

-Jonathan Sherwood, Roofers Helping Roofers

I DECLARE,
I HAVE ACCEPTANCE.

I am not average! I am a son (or daughter) of the most high King, Jesus. I am more than a conqueror in Christ. All my past is forgiven as far as the east is from the west. I am above and not beneath, the head and not the tail. I am special and extraordinary. Thank you, Holy Spirit for Your bright presence in me. Today, I am accepted into the Kingdom by You, Holy Father, and have been equipped and empowered to carry out Your will. This is my declaration. So be it. **Amen**

Reflection – Let your having become your doing...

What you think God thinks about is important. There is no shame for those whose accept Jesus as Lord, and Savior. Once you confess Him as Lord your life is redeemed from the curse of the law and legalism. You're in His family. You are his masterpiece. Do you accept yourself as a son or daughter of the King of the universe? How do you show acceptance to your employees? Your competition?

Have Gratitude for ACCEPTANCE:______________________________

____

Aspiring Goals for today:__________________________________

____

Victory I celebrated yesterday:____________________________

____

Expecting in Faith for:___________________________________

____

My Day 9 Character Builder

"For we are Gods masterpiece. He has created us new in Christ Jesus, so we can do the good things is He planned for us long ago." Ephesians 2:10

Day 10

I AM HUMILITY

Noun

1. a modest or low view of one's own importance; humbleness

"After a life of rock and roll in the 80's I decided I like staying off stage and remain hidden. I'm asking for a power greater than myself to do something that cannot be done by self-will or mere determination." -Roofers United, Jeff M. Richfield.

I DECLARE,
I HAVE HUMILTY.

I will obey Your instructions and cloth myself with Humility. I am a people builder looking to encourage others. I let others know they are highly valued calling out their greatness to help them rise above, and become all God created them to be. I shall remain hidden under the mighty arm of the Lord. I align myself to be the ladder to push others up higher. Today, I am keeping in constant check of the state of my heart and reflect upon my actions having and holding humility. This is my declaration. So be it. **Amen**.

Reflection – Let your having become your doing...

What kind of seeds are you planting in others? Do you allow others to be in the limelight? List a few examples how you let others know you admire them. How can you show it through an action today?

Have Gratitude for HUMILITY:____________________________

____

Aspiring Goals for today:__________________________________

____

Victory I celebrated yesterday:______________________________

____

Expecting in Faith for:___________________________________

____

____

	**My Day 10 Character Builder** *"Do nothing from selfish ambition or conceit, but in humility count others more significant than yourselves."* Philippians 2:3

Day 11

I AM WILLING

Noun

1. the quality or state of being prepared to do something; readiness

"Making a list of those harmed before coming into recovery may sound simple. Becoming willing to actually make those amends is the difficult part."

-Sam Hostetler, Five Star Roofing

I DECLARE,

I HAVE WILLINGNESS to see things from God's perspective.

I am a people builder looking to encourage others. I let others know they are highly valued calling out their greatness to help them rise above, and become all God created them to be. I shall remain willing to help, to teach, to give of my time talent and treasures. I cast off strife and remain open to the leading of Your spirit. Today, I am keeping in constant check of the state of my heart and emotions and pause to have and reflect willingness before I take action. This is my declaration. So be it. **Amen**.

Reflection – Let your having become your doing...

Do you tend to hold on to the past? Many of us get stuck in the past for your need for certainty or fear of the unknown. How can you loosen your grip on past behaviors that keep you spinning in circles so you and your business can stop coping and start winning?

Have Gratitude for WILLINGNESS:____________________________

____

Aspiring Goals for today:______________________________________

____

Victory I had yesterday:_______________________________________

____

Expecting in Faith for:____

____

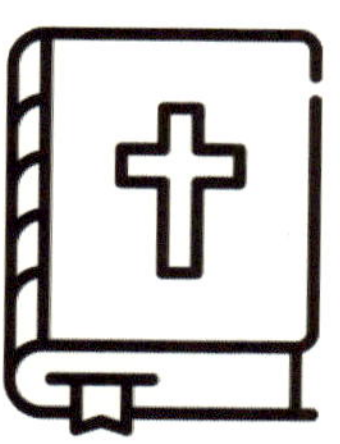	**My Day 11 Character Builder** *"Do nothing from selfish ambition or conceit, but in humility count others more significant than yourselves."* Philippians 2:3

Day 12

I AM FORGIVENESS

Noun

1. to stop feeling angry or resentful toward (someone) for an offense, flaw, or mistake. To cancel a debt.

"Deciding to forgive may sound simple. Becoming willing to actually make those amends is the difficult part."

Dr. David Miller, Rx Seed Coin,net

I DECLARE,
I HAVE FORGIVENESS.

Lord nothing is hidden from You. You are forgiving and good, abounding in love to all who call on You. I accept your grace and forgiveness that washes away all my sin. The blood of Christ made atonement for me and makes me whole again. The old life is gone, a new life has begun. I take my position in the heavens and bind the principalities and powers that operate against my life. Today, I am forgiving myself and others who have harmed me, to walk blameless before my heavenly Father. This is my declaration. So be it. **Amen**.

Reflection – Let your having become your doing...

I have found I need I forgive myself and others to maintain any real spiritual progress. I do this for my own sake first. Do you trust God enough to accept the forgiveness He offers. Close your eyes and ask the Lord if there is anyone from your past you need to forgive. Jot down any insights below then go make sure you make amends with sincerity of heart. I like to write a letter of amends to one even if I don't share it. How can you bring forgiveness to work where you've held resentment, anger or pride?

Have Gratitude for FORGIVENESS:____________________________

____

Aspiring Goals for today:____________________________________

____

Victory I celebrated yesterday:________________________________

____

Expecting in Faith for:______________________________________

____

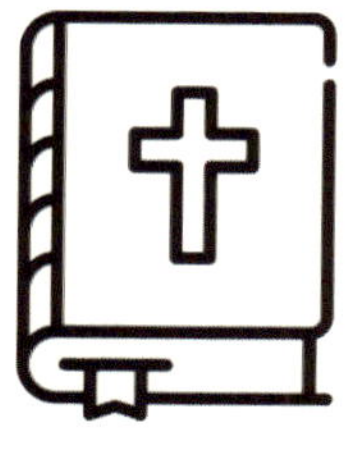

My Day 12 Character Builder

"And when you stand praying, if you hold anything against anyone, forgive them, so that your Father in heaven may forgive you your sins. Blessed is the one whose transgressions are forgiven, and whose sins are covered. Blessed is the man to whom the Lord does not impute iniquity, and in whose spirit there is no deceit." Psalm 32:1-2

Day 13

I AM OBEDIENT

Noun

1. compliance with an order, request, law or submission to authority Steadfast to reach a goal as in life or business by following direction.

"It's not natural to submit in the flesh, but in it we find fulfillment where life-long pursuits are carried out through dedication to obedience and to not cut corners."

- Stan Volkman, Contractors Alliance

I DECLARE,
I HAVE OBEDIENCE.

In Jesus name, I declare that the fruit of obedience shall be seen in my workplace. God has ordained favor for me as I walk in commitment. My strength is not determined by my own strength, but by my weakness; for when I am weak, I am strong in Christ. My heart shall remain steadfast to walk in Your will, and Your ways to manifest Your leadership at home and my office and those I am under authority Today, I am walking in obedience and have favor with God and man in compliance to Your Holy Spirit. Where You send me, Lord I will go. This is my declaration. So be it **Amen**.

Reflection – Let your having become your doing...

All companies have standards set in place that their employees are expected to follow. Being diligent and devoted workers respect company time and make it a point to remain busy while on the clock. How can you motivate your organization and employees to exemplify their obedience by honoring and respecting your standards?

Have Gratitude for OBEDIENCE:______________________________

____

Aspiring Goals for today:____________________________________

____

Victory I celebrated yesterday:________________________________

____

Expecting in Faith for:_____________________________________

____

My Day 13 Character Builder

"Jesus replied, Anyone who loves me will obey My teaching. My Father will love them, and He will come to them and make our home with them."
John 14:23

Day 14

I AM PRAYERFUL

Noun

1. address a solemn request or expression of thanks to God or other object of worship. A sacred act communing in solitude with God.

"There are times I don't know what to pray for. That's when I submit to the Holy Spirit Who intercedes for me with groans that words cannot express. He searches hearts and knows the mind of the spirit because You intercede for the saints in accordance with Gods will." - Jeff M Richfield, founder, Roofers United

I DECLARE,

I HAVE THE SPIRIT of prayer.

Lord, release the spirit of prayer over my life! Teach me how to pray the Fathers will for my business and employees. I am a priest over (your company name) and You are my spiritual CEO. I shall prayerfully lead (my company) to best of my ability and do everything in my capacity to honor You in our practices and dealings. You promised to help me succeed as I entreat others in prayer and seek for my client's success. My prayers availeth much and change things. I have faith for prayers that move mountains and heal the sick. Today, I am praying blessings of prosperity and life over my family, my employees, and my client's. This is my declaration. So be it. **Amen**.

Reflection – Let your having become your doing...

Through the power of prayer and meditation we begin to hear God and understand His ways. We dialogue with Him just as with your spouse or friends. As you understand him, you find the power to carry out His will and discover the plan He has for your life. Prayer is communion with the Creator of the universe who knows your smallest needs.

Have Gratitude for PRAYER:______________________________

____

Aspiring Goals for today:______________________________

____

Victory I celebrated yesterday:______________________________

____

Expecting in Faith for:______________________________

____

	**My Day 14 Character Builder** *"Pray in the Spirit without ceasing. Open up before God, keep nothing back; He'll do whatever needs to be done; He'll validate your life in the clear light of day and stamp you with approval at high noon. Quiet down before God and cryout aloud to Him."* Psalm 37:5, 1 Thessolonians 5:17

Day 15

I AM SERVANT

Noun

1. A means of delivering value to customers by facilitating outcomes customers want to achieve without the ownership of specific costs and risks. The action of helping or doing work for someone.

"When the best leaders achieve their purpose their employees claim the achievement as their own." -John Maxwell

I DECLARE,
I HAVE A SERVANT'S HEART.

Lord, manifest Your Spirit in me to serve. I have a license to serve in business and carry authority to serve in daily life. God is perfecting my servant leadership abilities right now. I speak to any spirit of disunity and I say be removed and cast away. I have been empowered by the Holy Spirit to serve and fulfill my destiny. I live to serve and jump at opportunities to administrate my gifting, my talents and time. Today, I am accepting the divine opportunities and appointments that have my name on them. This is my declaration. So be it. **Amen.**

Reflection – Let your having become your doing...

Professional service is the foundation of work ethic. Servant leadership begins at home and is the heartbeat of your company. Engage the law of reciprocity to your employees. Give positive feedback. Recognize achievements. In what ways have you exemplified "service" as one of the qualifiers of your organization? Do you respond quickly to clients?

Have Gratitude for SERVING:________________________________

____

Aspiring Goals for today:______________________________________

____

Victory I celebrate for yesterday:________________________________

____

Expecting in Faith for:____

____

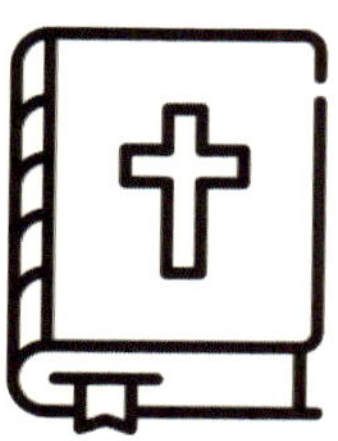

My Day 15 Character Builder

"For though I am free from all, I have made myself a servant to all, that I might win more of them. Every believer has received grace gifts, so use them to serve one another as faithful stewards of the many-colored tapestry of God's grace." Corinthians 9:19, 1 Peter 4:10

Day 16

I AM QUALIFIED

Adjective

1. Officially recognized as being trained to perform a particular job; certified.

"God doesn't call the qualified he qualified the called. You don't become qualified with God based on your performance, but you were MADE qualified by God when you received Jesus." - Steve Patrick

I DECLARE,
I HAVE BEEN QUALIFIED.

I am a partaker in the kingdom of God, saved by grace to do the work God's called me to do. I HAVE what I need to perform. Because I am qualified, I am justified. I do not have the spirit of fear, but of power, love and a sound mind. I overcome all because greater is He who is in me than he who is in the world. I am established in my workplace and righteousness and oppression is far from me. Today, I am keeping my head held high confident in this; that He who began a work in me will complete it until the day of Christ. This is my declaration. So be it. **Amen**.

Reflection – Let your having become your doing...

In what ways do you feel less than as a business owner? Do you see others in your industry and workplace as competition or in a cooperative spirit? Do you need training to feel confidence? In what ways are you qualified to mentor those less fortunate than you today?

Have Gratitude for being QUALIFED:________________________

____

Aspiring Goals for today:___________________________________

____

Victory I celebrate for yesterday:____________________________

____

Expecting in Faith for:____________________________________

____

____

My Day 16 Character Builder

"We give thanks to the Father, who has qualified you to share in the inheritance of the saints in the kingdom of light." Colossians 1:12

Day 17

I AM WISDOM

Noun

1. The quality of having experience, knowledge, and good judgment; the quality of being wise.

"When I look back at my early years, I see the mistakes made where I didn't take time to seek Godly counsel, but ran ahead without checking with others. And it cost me dearly." - Matthias Raber, Roofing Coach

I DECLARE,
I HAVE WISDOM.

The fear of the Lord is the beginning of wisdom, and all who follow Your precepts have good understanding. Teach me to fear You more, Lord. I roll my works upon You, and You make my thoughts agreeable to Your will. You direct my steps and make them sure. Spirit of the living God, restore sound wisdom for me. As I am upright; YOU are a shield to me as I walk in integrity, guarding my path with justice; YOU preserve my way as I AM godly; then I will discern righteousness and justice and equity and every good course. Today, I am wise and have the gift of knowledge, prudence and insight; so my plans shall be established and succeed. This is my Declaration. So be it. **Amen**.

Reflection – Let your having become your doing...

God holds success in store for the upright. King David and his son Solomon were men of great wisdom who sought the counsel of God for each decision they made. Only in disobedience to God can we fail to succeed. Don't be afraid to show others your faith in God. Make it a daily habit to seek God's wisdom and counsel from leaders around you. And remember that wisdom is to fear and revere the Lord.

Have Gratitude for WISDOM :____________________________________

____

Aspiring Goals for today:_______________________________________

____

Victory I celebrate in yesterday:__________________________________

____

Expecting in Faith for:____

____

My Day 17 Character Builder

"The Spirit of the LORD will rest on you-- the Spirit of wisdom and of understanding, the Spirit of counsel and of might, the Spirit of the knowledge and fear of the LORD." "For wisdom is a defense as money is a defense, But the excellence of knowledge is that wisdom gives life to those who have it." Isaiah 11:2, Ecclesiastes 7:12

Day 18

I AM VISION

Noun
As defined for your company-

1. The ability to think about or plan the future of a business with imagination or wisdom using your history to make your calling or purpose for life

---

"We Godpreneurs have had a moment in our life where God wants us to realize where our business is or if use for his purpose at our own. We all have a way in which God is going to use our past for his present and future."

-Alex Miranda. Founder, The Godpreneur

I DECLARE,
I HAVE VISION.

Lord, you speak to me personally so that my vision aligns with Yours. You are ever revealing and confirming the plans you have for me before I was even born. As I commit to walking out Your vision for my life, I walk out my high calling on earth. According to Hebrews 2:10, "Everything belongs to God." So today give me spiritual eyes to see any concerns with my job, my family, and finances, that may be at risk. Today, I am focused and have every spiritual blessing and earthly insight that pertains to my work-life vision. This is my declaration. So be it. **Amen.**

Reflection – Let your having become your doing...

The bible teaches where there is no vision the people die. The lord desires and declares He has prepared a future of welfare not destruction. Have you performed a S.W.O.T. analysis lately of the Strengths, Weaknesses, Opportunities, and threats to your organization? List some of these positives and negatives below.

Have Gratitude for VISION:____________________________________

____

Aspiring Goals for today:______________________________________

____

Victory I celebrate:____

____

Expecting in Faith for:_______________________________________

____

My Day 18 Character Builder

"Then the Lord answered me and said, 'Write the vision, and make it plain on tablets that he may run with it who reads it. For the vision is yet for an appointed time, and at the end it will speak and not lie. Though it tarries , wait for it because it will surely come and not tarry." Habakkuk 2

Day 19

I AM STEWARDSHIP

Noun

1. The job of supervising or taking care of something, such as an organization or property.

"Stewardship has to do with understanding that your life and business is not your own. I planted the seeds of my business and learned to take care of it, one day at time, God can water it and bring the fruit. God calls you to protect and nourish everything for his glory and the good of others." - April Hall, SRC SUMMIT

I DECLARE,
I HAVE STEWARDSHIP.

I present my business to You Lord and ask you to keep watch over it. The Lord protects me from all evil and guards my soul. In my heart are the highways of Zion. I go from strength to strength in the Lord. He gives me grace and glory. My Heavenly Father gives me the ability to be strengthened with his spirit in my inner man. I am steadfast immovable knowing that my toil is not in vain in the Lord. I am an heir with Jesus Christ. I am a royal priest and observing and doing the Lord's commandments. Today, I am strong in the Lord and have the strength of His might to overcome any obstacle. This is my declaration. So be it. **Amen.**

Reflection – Let your having become your doing...

God gives you the ability to see the needs in your business and clients and nurture that well even before the needs arise. Have you asked the Lord to show you the needs to be tended to? Ask God in a prayer to grant you stewardship over all that concerns you for today and jouranl.

Have Gratitude for STEWARDSHIP:______________________________

____

Aspiring Goals for today:____

____

Victory I celebrate for yesterday:__________________________________

____

Expecting in Faith for:____

____

My Day 19 Character Builder

"And God blessed them. And God said to them, "Be fruitful and multiply and fill the earth and subdue it and have dominion over the fish of the sea and over the birds of the heavens and over every living thing that moves on the earth." Genesis 1:28

Day 20

I AM DETERMINED

Noun

1. firmness of purpose; resoluteness. The quality of mind which reaches definite conclusions; decision of character; resoluteness. "To decree," "ordain," "mark out."

"Success in life is not about the car you drive, house you own, or money in the bank. When you close your eyes on this earth, all that will matter is the impact you made on those around you. We're you a positive force in the world?"

-Mikki Willis, Founder of Elevate and Plandemic the movie

I DECLARE,

I HAVE DETERMINATION.

My Father in heaven, grant unto me the spirit to persist even when it gets too difficult for me. Righteous God, Your Word says that hard work reaps profit and reward whereas only talk leads to poverty. My words and actions shall edify others and be an example how I plan to reach my goals. My God grants me divine strength to complete my course. I rejoice in my trust in You and give thanks that your angels are taking charge over me. Today, I am determined to do my very best at work so I shall reap a harvest of fruitfulness and prosperity. This is my declaration. So be it. **Amen**.

Reflection – Let your having become your doing...

Worshiping the Lord means you determine to present your body as a living sacrifice. Have you thought about presenting your business in a similar light? What areas do you have conflict between your plans and your people? How are you determined to lead by listening to the Spirit and seeking His will to be done today?

Have Gratitude for DETERMINATION:____________________

____

Aspiring Goals for today:____________________________

____

Victory I celebrate for yesterday:______________________

____

Expecting in Faith for:______________________________

____

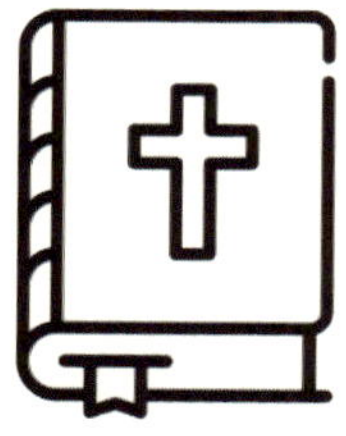	**My Day 20 Character Builder** *"Be on your guard; stand firm in the faith; be courageous; be strong. That is why, for Christ's sake, I delight in weaknesses, in insults, in hardships, in persecutions, in difficulties. For when I am weak, then I am strong. I can do all things through Christ who strengthens me."* - 2 Corinthians 12:10, 1 Corinthians 16:13, Phil 4:13

Day 21

I AM LOYAL

Adjective

1. giving or showing firm and constant support or allegiance to a person or institution; coming form the heart more than contract

"To go from good to great you need to be prepared to sacrifice. Loyalty is a mark of strong faith. Nothing worthwhile comes easy in this world. Those who get ahead build their life with true grit, courage, and hard work that comes with much sacrifice loyalty and pain." - James Richfield, Music City Roofers

I DECLARE,
I HAVE LOYALTY.

Lord, let the weight of Your glory support my spirit! I discipline my body and spirit to be a loyal team builder. I will look for ways to have fun at work while meeting my assignment. I am not a quitter but winner! You grant me endurance to bring me through today's challenges. For Thou has girded me with strength unto the battle; Thou has subdued under me those that rise up against me. I am living my best-self to inspire other people when life gets hard. Today, I am a loyal worker with Your divine grace and You have given me Your Spirit to rule and reign on the earth. This is my declaration. So be it. **Amen.**

Reflection – Let your having become your doing...

Empower your employees to become loyal building the trust factor. Meeting some basic needs of your employee ensures they remain loyal. It pays leaders to make business personal, emotional, mental, relational, physical, financial, purposeful and employable. How can you boost these dimensions and create meaningful trusting relationships today?

Have Gratitude for LOYATY:________________________________

____

Aspiring Goals for today:____________________________________

____

Victory I celebrate for yesterday:______________________________

____

Expecting in Faith for:______________________________________

____

My Day 21 Character Builder

"A man of many compaimons may come to ruin but there is one who sticks closer than a brother." Proverbs 18:24

Day 22

I AM RESPONSIBLE

Adjective

1. having an obligation to do something as part of one's job, role or position involving important duties, independent decision-making, or control over others.

"Never confuse faith and hard work. One goes hand in hand with the other. Retain faith that you will prevail in the end, regardless of the difficulties, while confronting head on the most brutal facts of your current reality." -The Stocksdale Paradox

I DECLARE,
I HAVE RESPONSIBILITY.

I am responsible when anyone anywhere reaches out for help. I want the hand of God to work though me. I take extreme ownership in my position and authority by God. I work as unto God for family, for my business, my church, my community, and my country which I serve. I don't make excuses, but I bring solutions. I take on the work I'm called to do with professionalism and excellence of spirit. It shows by what I produce as my clients get a righteous outcome. Today, I am established in God's Word and bring the Kingdom to my workplace. Kingdom of God come! This is my declaration. So be it. **Amen**.

Reflection – Let your having become your doing...

Personal responsibility is closely related to the law of sowing and reaping. Being willing to own our mistakes, confront our problems, and prepare for the worst. When you don't prepare for the worst the worst can win. List your three top plate business issues, and describe how will accomplish your goals by not being passive?

Have Gratitude for RESPONSIBILITY:____________________

____

Aspiring Goals for today:____________________________

____

Victory I celebrate for yesterday:_______________________

____

Expecting in Faith for:______________________________

____

My Day 22 Character Builder

"But if anyone does not provide for his relatives, and especially for members of his household, he has denied the faith and is worse than an unbeliever. Whatever you do, work heartily, as for the Lord and not for men." 1 Timothy 5:8, Colossians 3:23

Day 23

I AM ACCOUNTABLE

Adjective

1. (of a person, organization, or institution) required or expected to justify actions or decisions; responsible

---

"As a believer, I found I have everything within to create what I want out of life. I am first accountable to God, the Holy Spirit within for guidance and wisdom. That's where I find the strength to be accountable!" -Ephraim Glick, Conklin Coatings

I DECLARE,
I HAVE ACCOUNTABILITY.

Abba Father, I come to you as a son/daughter and declare your Lordship over me and my business! I do not walk in strife because I live in sonship with my Heavenly Father. I am victorious in my thoughts, my words, and my actions. I am attentive at work and hold my position with a sense of awe respecting myself and others. I will see You at work showing me how to respond to issues I face. Today, I am justified by faith and have You living in me working out all things together for my welfare. This is my declaration. So be it. **Amen**.

Reflection – Let your having become your doing...

Accountability lies at the heart of our work. It is a major key to living a life of victory. If we are to lead our team well we must be able to give an account, learn to apologize when wrong admit it, grow and move on. What mistakes have you owned up to? Do you have a coach or spiritual covering, someone who you submit to, and is praying for you?

Have Gratitude for ACCOUNTABILITY:____________________

Aspiring Goals for today:____________________________

____

Victory I celebrate in yesterday:________________________

____

Expecting in Faith for:______________________________

____

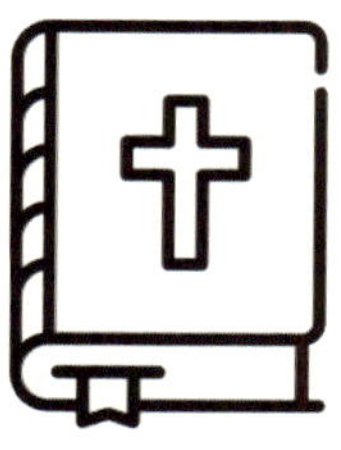	**My Day 23 Character Builder** *"For we must all appear before the judgment seat of Christ, so that each of us may receive what is due us for the things done while in the body, whether good or bad. As iron sharpens iron, so one person sharpens another."* 2 Corinthians 5:10, Proverbs 27:17

Day 24

I AM MEEK

Noun

1. the fact or condition of being meek; submissiveness

"The word meek from the original language was used to describe reining in a stallion. It is the idea of a horse being controlled by a bit and bridle. The horse is choosing to submit to authority. That is meekness. It is power under constraint."

-Pate Smith, MMA LAW, PLLC

I DECLARE,
I HAVE MEEKNESS.

Lord, Your Word is living and active in me. My influence wont stay small. Your power is at work under restraint. Jesus, You are meek and You sent Your Holy Spirit to live in me so we're living as one under Your authority. Therefore, I have meekness in me. You said I would do great works to glorify our Father. God brought me forth into a large place and delivers me because He delights in me. Your power is made perfect in my weakness. Let my platform increase and my busines flourish. Today, I am walking in meekness an have submitted to Your Lordship. This is my declaratio So be it. **Amen**.

Reflection – Let your having become your doing...

Meekness is a humble attitude that expresses itself in the patient endurance of offenses. It implies mercy and self-restraint. Meekness is not weakness. Sometimes we confuse the two. But the difference between a meek person and a weak person is this: a weak person can't do anything. A meek person, on the other hand, can do something but chooses not to. In business what ways have you had the power to judge or use force, but your confidence held you firm? How can you temper your anger using confident meekness?

Have Gratitude for MEEKNESS:______________________________

____

Aspiring Goals for today:_____________________________________

____

Victory I celebrate:____

____

Expecting in Faith for:______________________________________

____

My Day 24 Character Builder

"Take my yoke upon you, and learn from me, for I am gentle and lowly in heart, and you will find rest for your souls. Jesus said, "Blessed are the meek, for they shall inherit the earth" Matthew 11:29. 5:5

Day 25

I AM GENEROUS

Noun

1. of a person, showing a readiness to give more of something, as money or time, than is strictly necessary or expected. Showing kindness toward others.

"By choosing to willingly give what we can, to whoever we can, for as long as we can, we choose to create powerful moments in which we can connect with others using the talents God gave us. Anything less deprives those you come in contact with of an opportunity to glimpse the Kingdom of God."

- Coach Jim Johnson, Contractor Coach Pro

I DECLARE,
I HAVE GENEROSITY.

I am ONE with the giver and the gift. I am kind-hearted and bless others with no expectations. My light will so shine that others will see my good works and be acknowledged in heaven. God has given unto me exceeding great and precious promises to be a giver. I have taken on His nature, and have escaped selfishness, greed, and lust. I shall never be barren or unfruitful in the knowledge of the Lord and how to give. I am fruitful and give willingly to those in need. Today, I am giving and have all my needs met, pressed down, shaken together, and running over, for God loves a cheerful giver. This is my declaration. So be it. **Amen**.

Reflection – Let your having become your doing...

Generosity is our opportunity to serve the purpose of our Creator. God uses us a His tool to create abundance. Our time, our talents and our money are gifts we use to help others. Describe the last time you used your gift to bless another. How will you share your gifts today in a purposeful way expecting nothing in return?

Have Gratitude for GENEROSITY:______________________________

____

Aspiring Goals for today:______________________________________

____

Victory I celebrate:____

____

Expecting in Faith for:_______________________________________

____

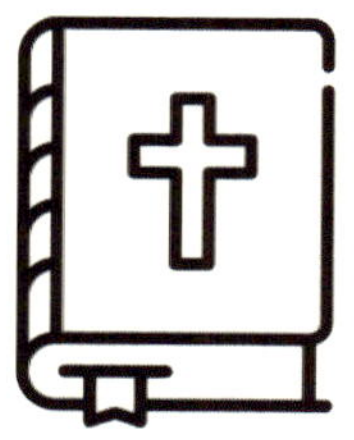

My Day 25 Character Builder

"Give, and it will be given to you: good measure, pressed down, shaken together, and running over will be put into your bosom. For with the same measure that you use, it will be measured back to you. The generous soul will be made rich, and he who waters will also be watered himself." Luke 6:38, Proverbs 11:25

Day 26

I AM COMPASSION

Noun

1. Sympathetic; pity and concern for the suffering or misfortune of others

---

"My philosophy on philanthropy & volunteering is a simple function of mathematics. If I wake up in the morning & the level of suffering in the world is X, when I got to bed at night, I want it to be X - 1. It is the difference between the two that expresses the value of my compassion & gratitude for how fortunate I have been in life."

-Doug Quin, Executive Director, American Policyholders Association

I DECLARE,
I HAVE COMPASSION.

Lord, You are a compassionate and gracious God, abounding in love toward me. Your compassion fails me not. The God of compassion is also the God of commerce. As I go forth today, You have given me power to profit, and subdue all matter of darkness and evil spirits. You make my spirit powerful to help heal the hurting, and to set prisoners free. Today, I am justified by faith to alleviate suffering, and have compassion toward everyone I meet. This is my declaration. So be it. **Amen**.

Reflection – Let your having become your doing...

The origin of the word helps us grasp the true breadth and significance of compassion. In Latin, 'compati' means "suffer with." Compassion means someone else's heartbreak becomes your heartbreak. Whom do you know who is suffering that you could pray for now, and stand beside later, maybe even without recognition?

Have Gratitude for COMPASSION:______________________________

____

Aspiring Goals for today:______________________________________

____

Victory I celebrate for yesterday:________________________________

____

Expecting in Faith for:____

____

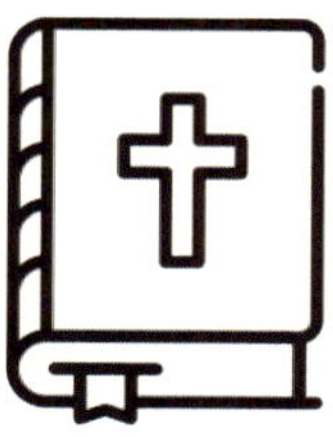

My Day 26 Character Builder

"Be kind and compassionate to one another, forgiving each other, just as in Christ God forgave you. Be like-minded, be sympathetic, love one another, be compassionate and humble." Ephesians 4:32, 1 Peter 3:8

Day 27

I AM PROVIDENT

Noun

1. the protective care of God or of nature as a spiritual power. Providing carefully for the future. Mindful in making provision.

"God's sovereignty is His right and power to do all that He decides to do."

-Reggie Brock, National accounts Manager, Beacon Building Products

I DECLARE,
I HAVE PROVIDENCE.

Lord, you have increased me more and more. My gates are continually open to the purposes of the Lord and cannot be thwarted. The forces of wealth in the marketplace come into my business in extravagant ways. Now is the time for the providence of God that has been stored up for me to be released in the name of Jesus. I meditate on the Word day and night, and whatever I do prospers. I am a generous and I fear the Lord, so I too will prosper. God's divine providence is given to me even in my sleep. God bestows wealth upon me because I love Him. Today, I am led by God's wisdom, and the providence I need to profit. This is my declaration. So be it. **Amen.**

Reflection – Let your having become your doing...

What do you understand by the providence of our Creator? All things in heaven, on the earth, and under the oceans continue to produce by Gods sovereign hand. Fruitful or barren years, rain or sunshine, all come not by chance but through His Fatherly hand. How can you rest knowing for today God has his eye on you, and will fulfill the desires of your heart as you meditate on His divine providence?

Have Gratitude for PROVIDENCE:__________________________

____

Aspiring Goals for today:___________________________________

____

Victory I celebrate:____

____

Expecting in Faith for:____________________________________

My Day 27 Character Builder

"And we know that for those who love God, all things work together for good, for those who are called according to His purpose. But remember the Lord your God, for it is he who gives you the ability to produce wealth, and so confirms his covenant, which he swore to your ancestors, as it is today." Romans 8:28. Deuteronomy 8:18

Day 28

I AM PATIENT

Noun

1. to the capacity to accept or tolerate delay, trouble, or suffering without getting angry or upset.

"In our challenges in the workplace we must remain undeterred and focused on our service toward our clients, and when things go wrong I've learned to bite my tongue more than speak." - Sam Struthers, Crest Roofing & Exteriors

I DECLARE,
I HAVE PATIENCE.

God has clothed me with patience. Even under trying circumstances, I discipline my thoughts and deny myself of giving in to impatience and irritability. I have learned to wait on You Lord as You renew my strength. When I am under strain, I will act with self-control and calmness. Instead of grumbling, I will speak of thanksgiving and praise. I will not be moved by what I see but what I know. Today, I am responding positively to situations and have patience to pause instead of reacting negatively. This is my declaration. So be it. **Amen.**

Reflection – The benefits of patience:

- Strengthens our ability to control our reactions, accept differences, and retain our peace of mind
- Enables us to make a calm and effective response to a challenging situation
- Prevents others getting hurt, when we are tempted to lash out in frustration, anger, or pain

What type of fast can you begin to start buffeting your patience?

Have Gratitude for PATIENCE:______________________________

____

Aspiring Goals for today:__________________________________

____

Victory I celebrate for yesterday:____________________________

____

Expecting in Faith for:___________________________________

____

My Day 28 Character Builder

"But those who wait on the Lord will renew their strength. They will soar on wings like eagles; they will run and not grow weary, they will walk and not be faint." Isaiah 40:31

Day 29

I AM AUTHENTIC

Adjective

1. of undisputed origin; genuine. A love for truth

"Discovering your authentic self is who you truly are as a person, regardless of your occupation, regardless of the influence of others, it is an honest representation of you. To be authentic means not being a people pleaser or caring what others think about you. Just be true to your heart and be your real self." - Bill Hicks, Hail Trace

I DECLARE,

I HAVE AUTHENTICITY.

Jesus release in me the truth of who You made me to be. I abide with You now Holy Spirit. My self-image is secure in Christ. I am transparent in all my business dealings. I do not brag and am not arrogant toward others. I'm not easily provoked and do not hold an offense. As a child of God, I am thoroughly furnished for good works. I rejoice with the truth and I am free of all falsehood. I am committed to God's love and ways. Today, I am an authentic disciple of Christ and have been set free of falsehood to be my word for such a time as this. So be it. **Amen**.

Reflection – Let your having become your doing...

Nine Powerful Ways Great Leaders Show Real Authenticity: They know who they are. They have high emotional intelligence. They know how to manage fear. They dream of a brighter future. They genuinely express themselves. They do not strive for perfection. They love and accept who they are. They always ask for second opinions. Which leadership quality will you chose to excel in today?

Have Gratitude for AUTHENTICITY:______________________________

____

Aspiring Goals for today:____

____

Victory I celebrate for yesterday:___________________________________

____

Expecting in Faith for:____

____

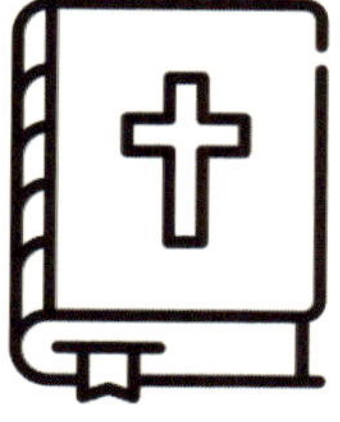	**My Day 29 Character Builder** *"Do your best to present yourself to God as one approved, a worker who has no need to be ashamed, rightly handling the word of truth. Let love be genuine. Abhor what is evil, hold fast to what is good."* 2 Timothy 2:15, Romans 12:9

Day 30

I AM RIGHTEOUS

Noun

1. the quality of being morally right or justifiable. One who believes God.

"We Godpreneurs have had a moment in our life where God wants us to realize where our business is or if use for his purpose at our own. We all have a way in which God is going to use our past for his present and future."

- Alex Miranda, Founder, The Godpreneur

I DECLARE,
I HAVE RIGHTEOUSNESS.

Father, I confess my belief in your Son, Jesus, as my Savior, therefore I am made the righteousness of God in Christ. I have been made righteous before my heavenly Father. God is going before me to make the crooked places straight. Since I have been made righteous through Christ, there is now no condemnation for me. My past is past. Today is a new day. The law of the Spirit of life in Christ Jesus has set me free from the law of sin and of death. I am righteous and flourish like the palm tree. Today, I am at peace, and have right standing with God and man. This is my declaration. So be it **Amen**.

Reflection –

When you gave your life to Christ He deemed you righteous. He removed all your shame. It can take years to realize that or it can take a seed of faith in a few seconds. With what level of certainty do you believe you stand free of all shame righteous before Christ? What's holding you back from living in fullness of faith?

Have Gratitude for RIGHTEOUSNESS:____________________________

____

Aspiring Goals for today:____

____

Victory I celebrate for yesterday:__________________________________

____

Expecting in Faith for:____

____

My Day 30 Character Builder

"Little children, let no one deceive you. Whoever practices righteousness is righteous, as he is righteous. Blessed are they who observe justice, who do righteousness at all times! Psalm 106:3, 1 John 3:7

Day 31

I AM KIND

Noun

1. of a good or benevolent nature or disposition, as a person being considerate

---

"Kindness is the new rich. People have good repoire with their clients when they are kind themselves as much as they care about others; people expect to be treated with respect and kindness."

-Morgan Walker, American Policyholders Association

I DECLARE,
I HAVE KINDNESS.

Remember me, oh Lord, with Your lovingkindess which is new each morning. You always treat me fairly. I am kind in relationships and compliment others even when undeserved. I am polite to everyone and generous with my belongings. I remember my manners and think of others well-being more than my own. I drink the cup of blessing and share kindness. Let Your beauty be shed upon my life to affect others. Today, I am the loving-kindness of God poured out over the brim of my heart to flow unto others. This is my declaration. So be it. **Amen**.

Reflection – Let your having become your doing…

Kindness means taking your positive loving energy and spreading it to the world, beginning with yourself. Kindness in business causes misunderstanding, mistrust, and hostility to evaporate. Kindness is caring for others even when they may not care for you. In today's reflection, journal who a name of someone who hurt you, and list a few examples how you could reflect kindness back to them.

Have Gratitude for KINDNESS:____________________________

____

Aspiring Goals for today:__________________________________

____

Victory I celebrate for yesterday:_____________________________

____

Expecting in Faith for:____________________________________

____

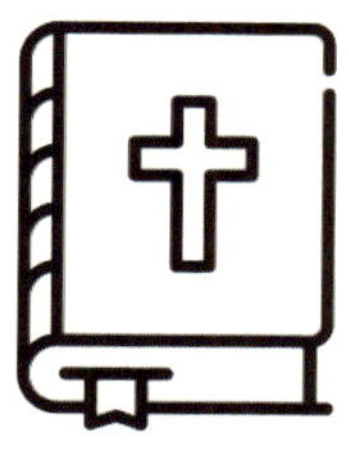	**My Day 31 Character Builder** *"And be kind one to another, tender-hearted, forgiving one another, even as God for Christ's sake hath forgiven you. But love your enemies, and do good, and lend expecting nothing in return, and your reward will be great, and you shall be sons of the most high, for He is kind to the ungrateful and the evil."* Ephesians 4:32, Luke 6:35

Day 32

I AM AMBITIOUS

Adjective

1. having or showing a strong desire and determination to succeed or achieve a particular goal

---

"My dad taught me that true modest ambition is not selfish gain or walking on others to get what you want, but that you live a peaceable, and quiet life that reflects power of character." - Reid Ribble, CEO NRCA

I DECLARE,
I HAVE AMBITION.

My core desire is driven and motivated by love. King of Glory, let your light break forth in my life as the morning dawn. I will put actions behind what You have placed in my heart. My God given purpose shall not be delayed, but is coming into alignment and with no delay. I am equipped to share the good God has done and placed in my heart. My ambition is to give You the glory. The Lord shall enlarge my tent pegs and stretch forth the curtains of my habitations. Today, I am committed to exploring new possibilities that leverage my faith to see my God-given goals come to reality. This is my declaration. So be it. **Amen.**

Reflection - Let your having become your doing...

The Bible speaks direct about doing nothing out of selfish ambition or vain conceit, but in humility consider others better than yourselves. If you are to reach your lofty business goals how then do you keep your ambition in check?

Have Gratitude for AMBITION:________________________________

____

Aspiring Goals for today:______________________________________

____

Victory I celebrate for yesterday:________________________________

____

Expecting in Faith for:____

____

My Day 32 Character Builder

"But we urge you, brethren, that you increase more and more; that you also aspire to lead a quiet life, to mind your own business, and to work with your own hands, as we commanded you, that you may walk properly toward those who are outside, and that you may lack nothing." 1 Thessalonians 4:11-12

Day 33

I AM PERSEVERING

Noun

1. persistence in doing something despite difficulty or delay in achieving success

---

"What makes a successful entrepreneur? Perseverance. It's where tenacity and believing in yourself and your team and your business is required. Indeed It's about not giving up and being the last man or woman standing when everyone else has fallen by the wayside."

- Steve Tobak, Author of "Real Leaders Dont Follow"

I DECLARE,
I HAVE PERSEVERANCE.

Lord, You're going forth is prepared as the morning, and You shall come as the rain, the latter and former rain upon my life. My gates are always open for blessings to come into my life. I will not be afraid but stay my course and PERSEVERE; for a great door has opened wide for me, though there may be opposition YOU make my enemies tumble! No difficulty will dissuade me from following what the Lord, Adonai has called me to do. Heaven is watching and rejoicing over me. Today, I am entrusted to the gracious care of Jehovah Jireh my Provider, for the work He has placed before me. This is my declaration. So be it. **Amen.**

Reflection – Let your having become your doing...

The Bible talks about not growing weary in well doing for in due season we will reap a harvest if we do not give up. How are you well able to persevere through the negative news, economic uncertainty, and the challenges facing your company? Ask God to pour out His Spirit on you.

Have Gratitude for PERSEVERANCE:____________________________

____

Aspiring Goals for today:____

____

Victory I celebrate for yesterday:__________________________________

____

Expecting in Faith for:____

____

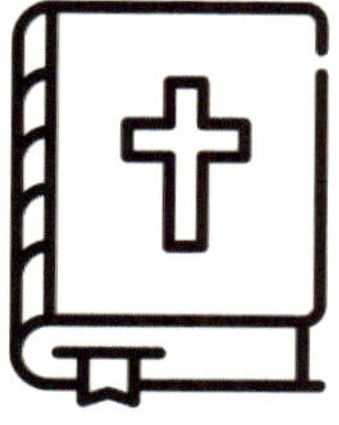

My Day 33 Character Builder

"But the Lord is faithful, and he will strengthen you and protect you from the evil one. And we are confident about you in the Lord that you are both doing – and will do – what we are commanding. Now may the Lord direct your hearts toward the love of God and the perseverance of Christ ." 2 Thessalonians 2:13-3:5

Day 34

I AM CONFIDENT

Noun

1. the feeling or belief that one can rely on someone or something: firm trust. a sense of self-assurance arising from one's appreciation of one's own abilities or qualities

---

"To have confidence as your top business strategy, you have to be okay with being yourself and live the story only you can. Embrace positivity, continue to grow and schedule time to play." - Will Sommer, Music City Roofers

I DECLARE,
I HAVE CONFIDENCE.

Father, I submit myself afresh to Your Spirit in unreserved confidence. Bless me at work with lasting peace confident You are with me. Having submitted to You, Lord, I perform as Your will directs fully assured that You see my labors and prosper me abundantly. I speak to every mountain in my life and command it to be removed and cast into the sea. I am seated with Christ in heavenly places far above all rule and principality. Today, I am not be afraid or dismayed, for I have my confidence and trust in You. This is my declaration. So be it. **Amen.**

Reflection- Let your having become your doing...

The word confidence is used 54 times in the King James Version and 60 times in the New International Version. The majority of uses concern trust in people, circumstances, or God. Where are you allowing your confidence to be swayed or influenced by others rather than by God? Are you able to keep your cool in an argument?

Have Gratitude for CONFIDENCE:____________________________

____

Aspiring Goals for today:____________________________________

____

Victory I celebrate for yesterday:_____________________________

____

Expecting in Faith for:______________________________________

____

My Day 34 Character Builder

"Though an army encamp against me, my heart shall not fear; though war arise against me, yet I will be confident. The Lord will fulfill his purpose for me; your steadfast love, O Lord, endures forever. Do not forsake the work of your hands." Psalm 27:3, Psalm 138:8

Day 35

I AM CULTURE

Noun

1. the customs, arts, social institutions, of human intellectual achievements of a particular nation, people or other social group

---

"Most people think that culture is a thing but actually it's an experience. What type of experience do you want your team to have? When making decisions think about the team experience."

- Dr. Jessica Stahl, Owner, Ignite Results

I DECLARE,
I HAVE CULTURE.

Lord, You deeply care for our culture. I speak words of faith over the leaders of our industry and our nation. Let my company and our industry always promote justice and righteousness. May business owners stand for truth and let them rule by the fear of the Lord. May we learn to serve our clients and communities by maintaining core values, respecting relationships, taking responsibility, providing transparency, garnering stewardship, and living to serve. Today, I am upholding the good reputation of our industry worldwide and have become a voice to spread the message of hope and restoration. It is our unbreakable unity that will create the change we wish to see. This is my declaration. So be it. **Amen.**

Reflection- Let your having become your doing...

In our workplace we need to be observant to be the culture of our Christianity in hope we will keep this sound foundation. For this is the bedrock which Christ built His church, and this is the culture we live and believe is here to set the world right. How will you carry on living a Christian culture in the midst of the coming new world order?

Have Gratitude for CULTURE:____________________________

____

Aspiring Goals for today:________________________________

____

Victory I celebrate for yesterday:___________________________

____

Expecting in Faith for:__________________________________

____

My Day 35 Character Builder

"While God has overlooked the times of human ignorance, now He commands all people everywhere to repent, because He has fixed a day on which He will have the world judged in righteousness by a Man whom He has appointed, and of this He has given assurance to all by raising Him from the dead." Acts 17:30-31

Day 36

I AM BREATH

Noun

1. the air taken into or expelled from the lungs.

"The key to consistent growth is to stay above water, keep in relationship with God and others (keep breathing), and most of all trust God when the tide is low. Realize GOD put people in your life for His good will to be done. Love - lead - laugh ......and breath deep!

-Troy Clymer, President – The Catalyst Group

I DECLARE,
I HAVE BREATH.

Discover the power of vital breathing. Today is an exercise.

Take 10 power breaths into the deepest part of your lungs by inhaling for eight seconds hold for 10 seconds exhale for 16 seconds. As you breath in think of the words, HOPE, FAITH, LOVE IN! Repeat these words as you breath in.

As you exhale let the negative energy out. On the exhale you might repeat these words: FEAR, HURT, PAIN. GONE!

The idea is to keep on filling you your tank with positive energy and release any negative energy. On the last breath you can make a SHOUT of joy using a "YAH!" or phrase of your own. This exercise removes bad feelings and gives your heart and mind the fuel to start the day in victory!

Reflection – Let your having become your doing...

The Lord says, "My Spirit has made you, and the breath of the Almighty gives you life." How did your emotional state change after the exercise? Did you feel any state of depression or fatigue leave your body?

Have Gratitude for BREATH:______________________________

____

Aspiring Goals for today:______________________________

____

Victory I celebrate for yesterday:______________________________

____

Expecting in Faith for:______________________________

____

____

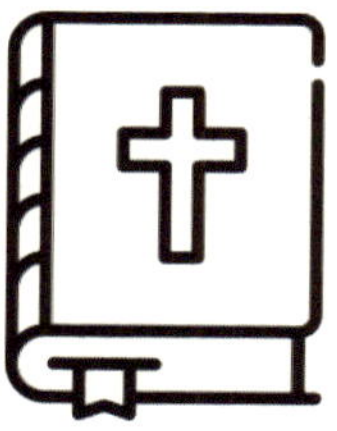

My Day 36 Character Builder

"Then the LORD God formed man of the dust of the ground, and breathed into his nostrils the breath of life; and man became a living being." Genesis 2:7

Day 37

I AM LEGACY

Noun

1. the richness of an individual's life, including what they left behind and the impact he or she had on people and places

---

"We often think we're building a company, but what we're really building is a legacy. We are putting a stamp on the future and making a contribution for generations. In this way we feel our life matters."

-Nicki Brewster, Director of Operations, Music City Roofers

I DECLARE,
I HAVE LEGACY.

I am called in Christ to live a faith-filled legacy. Favor is on my life because of the Lord. I break all assignments of the enemy against my finances in the name of Jesus. By following You, Lord, my legacy will be fulfilled. I am God's servant, and He takes pleasure in my prosperity. I love wisdom and inherit substance and my treasures are filled. Lord, open the floodgates of heaven over my life that my barns be filled with plenty. Today, I am living my legacy and have a prospering business. Lord let your covering protect me all the days of my life. This is my declaration. So be it. **Amen**.

Reflection – Let your having become your doing...

Legacy isn't defined by how much money we make, but money is often a byproduct of leaving a legacy. But the real legacy is the lives you touch and help change along the way that make a lasting change! People will forget what you said, but they will never forget how you made them feel! What milestones are you leaving behind so when you're gone people will see the greatness you left behind?

Have Gratitude for LEGACY:______________________________

____

Aspiring Goals for today:______________________________

____

Victory I celebrate for yesterday:______________________________

____

Expecting in Faith for:______________________________

____

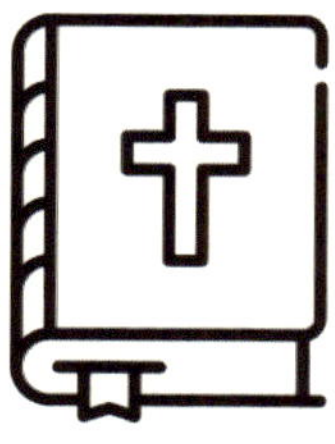

My Day 37 Character Builder

"A good man leaves an inheritance to his children's children, but the sinner's wealth is laid up for the righteous. One generation shall commend your works to another, and shall declare your mighty acts." Proverbs 13:22, Psalm 145:4

Day 38

I AM X FACTOR

Noun

1. a variable in a given situation that could have the most significant impact on the outcome.

"So what can you do to get the X Factor in your small business? Simply, make it a priority. That means believing in your brand, your people and your customers."

\- Joe Hughes, Contractor Dynamics

I DECLARE,
I HAVE "X FACTOR."

I dwell in the secret place of the Most High! I receive abundance of grace and I reign in life through Jesus Christ. You shall bring to pass those things hidden in my heart. This is the day of my salvation. I shall decree a thing and shall be established in my life. I have favor with God and man. The Spirit of God is multiplying and strengthening my talents and gifts in the workplace. You will make all grace abound toward me so that I will have sufficiency in all things and abound to every good work. Today, I am carrying the X Factor of the Spirit of the Lord and have his light which makes me shine bright for the world to see. This is my declaration. So be it. **Amen**.

Reflection – Let your having become your doing...

An X factor in business is the ability to add intangible value to your product or service. It's finding a way to do more for your clients than any of your competitors and consistently maintaining that standard. List five ways your company goes the extra mile. What's your X-Factor?

Have Gratitude for my X FACTOR:______________________________

____

Aspiring Goals for today:____

____

Victory I celebrate for yesterday:___________________________________

____

Expecting in Faith for:____

____

	My Day 38 Character Builder *"But you are a chosen race, a royal priesthood, a holy nation, a people for his own possession, that you may proclaim the excellencies of him who called you out of darkness into his marvelous light."* 1 Peter 2:9

Day 39

I AM HOLY

Noun

1. dedicated or consecrated to God or a religious purpose; worthy of the divine; sacred or set aside for the Lord. "the Holy Bible"

Holiness is the character of God. The purpose of God and salvation of mankind is to produce in man a kindred holiness a radiant purity like unto that of God himself.

I DECLARE,
I HAVE HOLINESS.

I am set apart as holy unto the Lord. I choose to obey God in every area of my life through my outward actions as well as my inward thoughts, and motives of my heart. I renounce all sin, pride, lust, idolatry, perversion, immorality, gluttony, envy and slothfulness. I yield my body and its passions to the Holy Spirit's authority. I put my body, the temple of God, into subjection so that I will not bring a reproach to the gospel. Today, I am protecting my virtue and have been appointed and anointed by the Holy Spirit dwelling in me. This is me declaration. So be it. **Amen.**

Reflection – Let your having become your doing...

The Holy Spirit unveils your desire of the flesh, and your adverse tendencies as part of His purpose for growth in Gods plan for your life. How can the nature of man be changed except that his nature is first revealed? How are you taking steps to expel evil desire? Do you make plans without asking God the Holy Spirit what He thinks? How are you consciously permitting the Spirit of God to be your absolute guide?

Have Gratitude for HOLINESS:____________________________

____

Aspiring Goals for today:________________________________

____

Victory I celebrate for yesterday:___________________________

____

Expecting in Faith for:__________________________________

____

My Day 39 Character Builder

"In the last days it will be, God declares, that I will pour out my Spirit upon all flesh, and your sons and your daughters shall prophesy, and your young men shall see visions, and your old men shall dream dreams, but as He who called you is holy, you also be holy in all your conduct, because it is written. "Be holy. for I am holy."

Day 40

I AM SHALOM

Noun

1. used as salutation by Jewish people at meeting or parting, meaning "peace." The Blessings of God and the way it's supposed to be.

Shalom (Hebrew: שָׁלוֹם shalom) is a Hebrew word and is much more than a casual social greeting— it is a prayer, a blessing, a deep desire, and a benediction. It is a word that is packed with the full blessing of God. It's the way life is supposed to be."

-Bob Perry, Workplace Prayer

I DECLARE,
I HAVE SHALOM.

Jesus, (Yeshua), You are the Prince of peace. I receive this word with faith to walk forth with POWER in this world. I repent of limited thinking. I break all limitations on my life. Holy Spirit of God, (RUACH HAKODESH) I bind the principalities and powers that operate against my life and business. I dispatch Angelic troops to surround my family, my business, and the land I dwell in to deliver the Shalom of the Lord. Bring forth inner wholeness to everyone in my sphere of influence. From this day forth, I am alive with passion, purpose, authority, and praise knowing I was destined for this time to be the salt and light in the earth. This is my eternal exchange. This is my declaration. So be it. **Amen**.

Reflection – Let your having become your doing...

Deeper translations of Shalom meaning peace, salvation, harmony, wholeness, completeness, prosperity, welfare, reconciliation, and tranquility can be used idiomatically to mean both hello and goodbye.

It is in this final day 40, that I say goodbye by choosing to speak "Shalom!" over you, in all life, freedom, and inner wholeness over you, your family and your business. This 40-day journey is a small moment in time, but it's my sincere desire you continue to use the power of God's Word to script your life and reach your high calling. For this final day of your journey meditate on gratitude and thankfulness of your accomplishment. Sign your commitment of pledge on the following pages and return them. I would love to hear how this impacted you.

Have Gratitude for SHALOM:______________________________

____

Aspiring Goals for today:___________________________________

____

Victory I celebrate for yesterday:_____________________________

____

Expecting in Faith for:_____________________________________

My Day 40 Character Builder

Jesus says, "Peace I leave with you; my peace I give you. I do not give to you as the world gives. Do not let your hearts be troubled and do not be afraid." John 14:27

Congratulations on your commitment to the Character Challenge. Review, sign, and snap a photo of these pledges and return to me at: admin@musiccityroofers.com and I'll be praying for you...

Full Circle "Wheel of Character" in the Marketplace

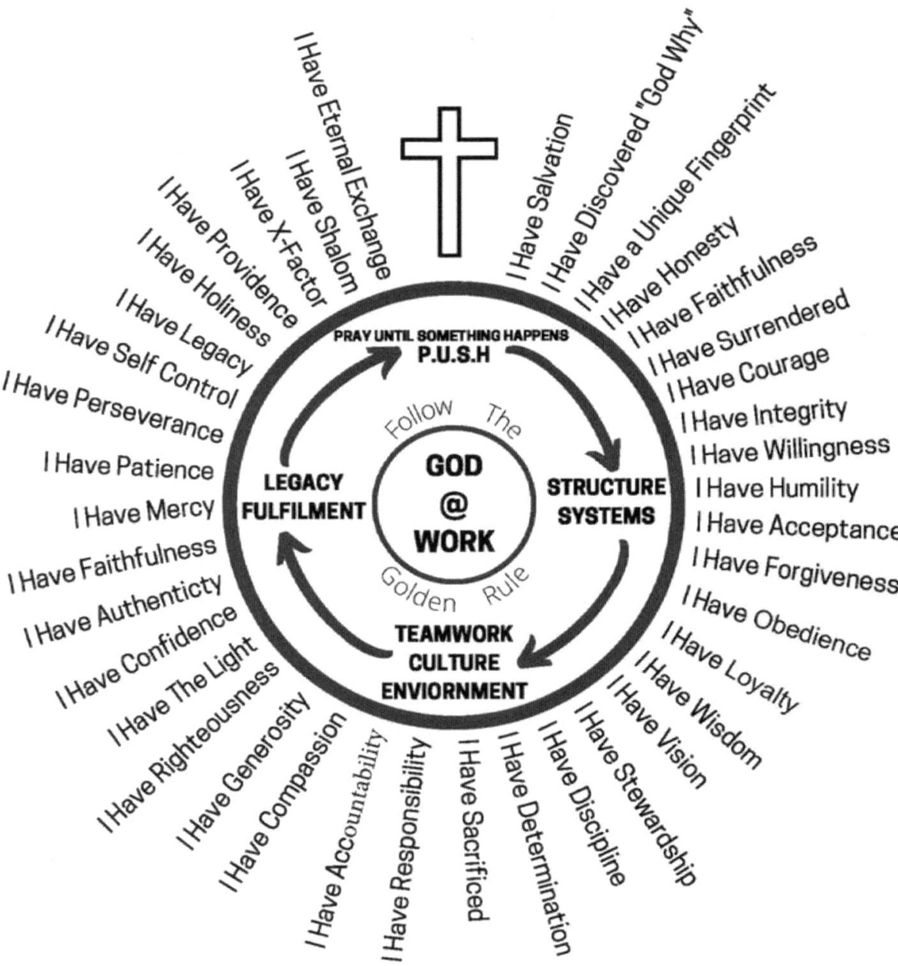

When you put God @ Work as the center of all your Dream, then add Faith + Action = Legacy

This is The Eternal Exchange

Sign below as a record of remembrance of fulfillment of your 40 days of character.

Signature

Example of Prayer to Cover Your Businesses

Lord, You store up sound wisdom for the upright; You are a shield to me and I walk in integrity, guarding my path. Then I will discern righteousness, justice and EVERY good course. Wisdom has entered my heart, knowledge is pleasant to my soul; discretion guards me, understanding watches over me to deliver us from evil. I ask for a fresh outpouring of Your Holy Spirit, that the UNITY of Christ would overtake us and that we would be as One with You.

Divine Protection: NO accidents shall befall us. NO harm will overtake us. Protect my teams from all disease, Covid, Cancer, viruses, accidents and terror. Keep us healthy and whole to stay equipped to earn a livelihood for our families to thrive.

Divine Team: God send us the right people to fill our seats who are teachable and work hard to serve and win! Help us scale in Your timing.

Divine Providence: God bestows wealth on those who love Him making their treasuries full. You give to Your beloved even as we sleep! Much wealth is in the house of the righteous.

Divine Revelation: Let me hear Your voice as CEO of my businesses. Lead and guide me to lead my people. Show me things to be known to keep us safe and whole. Leave no rock unturned to serve my clients so they have a righteous outcome.

Divine Help: From the Sovereign Lord comes escape from destruction. God daily bares our burdens. For the wages of the righteous is LIFE!

Lord, help me not to overlook any client needs, nor to be taken advantage of, but be prompt in all my dealings that my clients have the best service and outcome from me/ us. Do not forsake me Lord, leave nothing to chance, show me all hidden matters, that we experience no loss. Grant us unity to win as an effective efficient team to fulfill our high calling in this city that Your name be glorified, Your Kingdom come and reign over our city, in Yeshua's mighty name! AMEN.

DECLARE THIS PRAYER FROM YOUR POSITION IN HEAVEN!

Abba Father, in the name of Jesus, I rise early to declare Your Lordship over me and my family and business! I get under the covering of the shadow of Your Wings El Shaddai and anointing. I come in agreement with the heavens that declare Your Glory. Father, please release the mysteries unto me to bring heaven down to earth. Thank You that the (angels) are battling on my behalf. Your Kingdom come and I declare YOUR will be done on earth as it is in Heaven!

My appointed times have been set by You Yahweh in the heavens; therefore I declare words of life that will make contact with the womb of the morning and make her pregnant with life and purposes designed by You Yahweh. I declare in Jesus' name that at sunrise the dawn gives birth to the will of YahWeh Elohim, and light shines on wickedness to shake it and destroy it from the heavens. At twilight my enemies flee, and newly found spoils await me at my destination. My God given destiny is inevitable!

O Jehovah let my prayers meet You today. I command the morning to open its ears unto me and hear my cry. Let conception take place so that prayer will rain down and angels be dispatched upon the earth to Your will. Lift up your heads, Oh you gates be lifted up you ancient abiding doors that the KING of Glory my come in, the King of Glory Jehovah Sabboath, strong and mighty in battle!

In Jesus name I declare that the first fruit of my morning is Holy, and the entire day will be Holy. I prophesy the will of Yah to the morning so that the first light will shake wickedness from the four corners of the earth. The lines (my portion) are fallen on my behalf in pleasant (sweet, agreeable) places, and I have a secure heritage in Christ Jesus.

I am strategically lined up with the ladder that touches the third heaven and sits on earth. The angels are descending and ascending according to the works that I speak. What I bind or Forbid and loose or Permit on earth is already bound or loosed in heaven. Today, I release revelation, healing, deliverance, salvation, peace, joy, wealth and abundance to my sphere of influence in Christ name! Be glorified Yeshua!

JOIN THE MOVEMENT

"Pledge to be a Voice for the Roofing industry!"

In order to bring clarity of purpose we're asking each roofer and affiliate to conduct business in an ethical manner and commit to the **Roofer's Reformer Pledge** as a qualification to join our vibrant UNITED community.

I commit to:

Be a Voice. Promote unity within Roofers United and be a voice of reformation upholding the state of the roofing industry at large, and linking arms with causes who align with our vision like APA, and The Catalyst Group.

Maintain our Core Values. Integrity, Transparency, Servant-Leadership, Unity, Collaboration, and Empowerment are the values that shall make our community thrive.

Respect Relationships. Treat customers and vendors in a professional and timely manner. Protect the rights of your co-workers, subcontractors and those you work with. When you make a mistake own it, apologize, do what is right even if it comes with a cost.

Take Responsibility. Design, install and operate with purpose in a manner compatible with public health, safety, and environmental values. Employ or engage well-trained personnel. Offer and honor clear, understandable warranties that comply with all applicable laws and regulations. Strive to be safe on the job, drive with caution, and be respectful of others on the road.

Provide Transparency. Educate clients with insurance scopes without undue influence. Conform to the law and intent of federal, state and local incentives and fairly represent the impact of such that may hinder or hurt our industry.

Garner Stewardship. Never work for free unless by charity, nor give away deductibles as this would erode the value of our industry. Do good work for a profit but not at the cost of integrity being willing to walk away from a job if it is not compatible with your values or mission.

Live to Serve. Generosity creates a culture of unity and freedom and the thriving culture we desire. Do whatever it takes to get help the job done and then some. Create an extraordinary experience for your clients and loyalty is what you'll earn.

Carry the Message. Uphold the good reputation of roofers worldwide, and spread the message to restore the roofing industry to wholeness. Be an active member of our community. It is our unbreakable Unity that will create the change we strive for.

______________________________________ _______________

Signature of Authorized Representative Date

ABOUT THE AUTHOR

Jeff M. Richfield is a devoted husband, and father, a champion of prayer and motivation and serves citywide ministries. As a General Contractor, he owns Music City Roofers, LLC, a thriving roofing culture, and is founder of Roofers United, a nonprofit devoted to spiritually investing in the lives and legacies of leaders in the marketplace through mentoring and equipping business leaders.

As a seasoned entrepreneur, and gifted writer, Jeff is on the advisory board of RX SEEDCOIN.NET, "The Coin of Compassion" that is usir the blockchain to tokenize acts of compassion to serve and solve the issues of Hunger, Homelessness, and Health. Download a digital wallet to learn more: www.RXSeedCoin.net.

Along with a committed team of ministry partners Jeff is helping build a 70-acre campus of compassion, Eagles Landing, a sovereign community c compassion, to grow community gardens, help the hurting, and equip the next generation with the Good News of the Gospel of Christ. Learn mor at www.HarvestSoundInternational.com.

Jeff lives with his wife, Jodi, on their farm outside Nashville, TN., a have two amazing boys (now men - loving life), a few spiritu daughters, four horses they never ride, and a host of surprising fu loving animals on their farm where devotion to prayer and solitude expressed.

Among his favorite things are playing the piano in the woods, running t dog or the dog running him, playing drums to his favorite beat, a finding solitude to listen, pray, and create.

In addition to building his own companies and developing commun transformation Jeff coaches entrepreneurs privately. For speaki engagements you may connect with him at www.MusicCityRoofers,cc or www.RoofersUnited.com to schedule a discovery call.